Intelligence in the Digital Age

Intelligence in the Digital Age

How the Search for Something Larger May Be Imperiled

Lyn Lesch

ROWMAN & LITTLEFIELD
Lanham • Boulder • New York • London

Published by Rowman & Littlefield
An imprint of The Rowman & Littlefield Publishing Group, Inc.
4501 Forbes Boulevard, Suite 200, Lanham, Maryland 20706
www.rowman.com

6 Tinworth Street, London SE11 5AL

ISBN 9781475854572 (cloth)
ISBN 9781475854589 (paperback)
ISBN 9781475854596 (electronic)

British Library Cataloguing in Publication Information Available

Library of Congress Cataloging-in-Publication Data

Library of Congress Control Number: 2019949765

For my father and mother

Contents

Acknowledgments

I am grateful to my editor at Rowman & Littlefield, Tom Koerner, who was willing to take a chance on publishing this very different, offbeat book whose subject matter does not yet entirely exist in the modern world. I am also grateful to Jim Wasner, Bill Pollack, and Renee and Dave Porter for the numerous discussions I have had with them over the years relative to the topics included in this book, discussions that helped to sharpen my own focus. I am likewise grateful to my sister-in-law Sheryl Lesch, whose enthusiasm for and support of both my writing and my life has always meant so much to me. Above all, I am grateful to my brother Chip Lesch, who gave me constant support and encouragement to pursue this project and also provided me with any number of books and articles for research purposes. Without his continued assistance and support, this book might very well have never come to fruition.

Chapter One

The Search for Something Larger in a New Age

The late Neil Postman—media critic, communications theorist, long time professor at New York University, and the author of such important works as *The Disappearance of Childhood* and *The End of Education*—once wrote that there are two important questions one must ask whenever any new, unforeseen technology comes into existence: What present problems does it solve? And what new problems does it create?

Postman died in 2003, but he was certainly around long enough to see the pervasive influence of the personal computer on all our lives and so was able to write some splendid critiques concerning our new Internet age. He was unfortunately gone by the time two important new adjuncts to this situation came into existence, these of course being the rapid rise of social media sites such as Facebook and Twitter and the invention of the iPhone.

The first development, the advent of social media, has obviously led to an interconnected world of instant communication where people without much domestic currency in a particular area of endeavor are able to effortlessly connect with those who are in fact actual icons in that area at the same time that it has made it possible to by and large connect with anyone whom one chooses just as long as they decide to respond.

At times it is easy for one to imagine that he or she is part of one large, inclusive cyber brain in which there are no longer any secrets, and where time and space are reduced to meaningless constructs that can be negotiated with just one click of the mouse on one's computer or one touch on one's smartphone screen.

The second development, the iPhone, initially announced by Steve Jobs at the MacWorld Convention on January 9, 2007, has made it possible to literally carry that interconnected cyber world with us at all times. And as that interconnectedness has become mobile through the seemingly magical use of one's phone to immediately access Facebook, Twitter, or any other social media site, or to text or email one's friends or acquaintances, we (or at least those of us who are not digital natives) are now experiencing a new world, in which one can move through one's daily life without ever really being out of touch with anything or anyone with whom one is significantly interested. And this is possible at a speed many people still find breathtaking.

Yet at the same time, despite this incredible new age of immediate interconnectedness that few of us had been able to see coming, it seems important to return to the two questions that Neil Postman believed it was important to ask at the dawn of any new age: What previous problems, if any, has this new digital age solved, and what new problems has it created?

Certainly, the age of having to travel to the local library to retrieve information concerning a subject in which one might be interested, looking for the nearest payphone when one is out and about in the world without access to a phone in one's car, or spending significant amounts of time and energy to track down someone from one's chosen profession with whom one needs to communicate around certain important issues is now over, all of these previous inconveniences having now been obliterated by the possibility of immediate connection that the Internet and our digital devices have made available.

Now that we have grown used to these connections with others in cyberspace, few classroom teachers would think of making a trip to the local library late in the evening to hunt down information for a lesson the following day when all they have to do is Google it on their computer.

The idea of looking for payphones that no longer exist now that everyone has a smartphone is now a thing of the past, and having to make a number of phone calls or send letters by mail to attempt to contact a significant person with whom one wishes to communicate professionally would be deemed an annoying inconvenience now that one can either email or text that person, or perhaps attempt to communicate with him or her on social media.

So in a certain sense, our digital age has solved the problem of slow communication in a world that is moving ever faster. Likewise, of course, there are other ways in which our new Internet age has made all our lives easier. One thinks immediately of such things as GPS trackers in one's car while negotiating city traffic or during long road trips, paying for items with one's phone rather than having to always carry cash, or even being able to immediately pull up the name of some famous person, invention, movie, or band while discussing various aspects of our culture at a dinner party with friends.

Yet, at the same time, there is the second question that Neil Postman posited to all of us: What new problems might this new digital age of ours have created? Here, it would seem, the answers are not so obvious. Some of them have to do not only with specific aspects of our everyday lives, such as how we might have lost a certain expectation of privacy and protection from fraudulent activities we had before the dawn of the Internet, but also with how the Internet and digital devices that are now so fully a part of our existence might be in fact negatively impacting our attention spans and other mental functions.

Fortunately, more and more is now being written and researched concerning this latter issue in terms of the length of our attention spans, our capacity for deep reading of significant articles and books, our working memories, and even our ability to think and learn creatively. Increasingly, one finds oneself coming across articles in magazines and newspapers or programs on cable television that deal with the issue of Internet addiction or how our use of smartphones, tablets, and PCs might be affecting our mental capabilities, particularly our attention spans and memories.

Although it is certainly not something that is now on most people's radar screens, there is also the issue of consciousness expansion. That is, the transcendence of self in pursuit of a larger awareness, a pursuit that is very much a matter of looking closely at the structure of one's thinking mind, the self, the potentially illusory nature of memory and the past, or the relationship of knowledge itself to all of these.

It involves the realization that unless one possesses a certain subtlety of mind, it would appear to be all but certain that the possibility of investigating a more expansive intelligence in any clear-sighted way is not only nearly impossible but also might lead toward serious mental confusion.

As much as anything, this is a journey that begins with examining one's own conditioning until one begins to realize, as the late philosopher-thinker Jiddu Krishnamurti often said, "You are the world." Or with the realization of which Fritjof Capra wrote in his groundbreaking book *The Tao of Physics*—namely, that the basic oneness of the universe is not only one of the most profound revelations of modern physics but also a central characteristic of the mystical experience in relation to our own lives.

And for these type of realizations to take place, it would seem, one must have both focused attention and clear access to one's short- and long-term memories, combined with the capacity to step outside of these, and even on occasion step outside one's rational mind itself to look clearly at the actual process of thought or the intrinsic nature of the self.

This might be one of the real dangers of succumbing to the sort of digitally enhanced distracted awareness and memory loss about which any number of neuroscientists and researchers are now warning us—that, lost in a thicket of bits of information relentlessly coming at us on the Web, we might begin to lose a certain amount of our capacity for self-reflection, as well as the ability to put the atomized bits of knowledge one encounters in cyberspace into the sort of larger conceptual framework that allows us to closely examine our own minds and memories in relation to them.

It is hard to imagine how someone could actually travel the path toward a larger, more expansive awareness, one that might actually begin to transcend the boundaries of rational thought while inhabiting one's normal state of mind if they are the victim of a distracted attention in which they have lost much of their capacity for serious self-reflection concerning their thoughts and memories.

Yet if a potentially deleterious relationship exists in a distracted attention that is potentially being engendered in us by the effects that our digital technologies and the Internet might be provoking, it seems necessary that we begin by looking specifically at the possible effects that our use of digital technologies may be having on our cognitive capacities in relation to the search for a larger intelligence.

In addition, as important as investigations of how the digital world might be affecting us in a manner in which deep concentration and the ability to think creatively are being compromised are, it seems likewise important that we begin to understand how our current Internet age may be having a similar deleterious effect on the intuitive, subtle nature of our mental processes, those which are necessary for fully comprehending the workings of our minds and selves while searching for a more expansive awareness concerning ourselves and our world.

Chapter Two

Digital Minds

As cognitive theorists, medical researchers, and neuroscientists have begun to study the effects that the virtual world may be having on our minds and brains—particularly the minds and brains of those in their formative years—greater and greater attention is being paid to the possibility that how we use our digital devices may be actually changing our entirely malleable brains in a manner that affects our attention spans, our capacity to learn, and our ability to be creative.

To this end, any number of books and articles have now been written on the subject, discussing specifically how our addictive use of smartphones, computers, and tablets may be negatively affecting our brains in a manner in which they are undergoing profound changes in order to adapt themselves to our new digital universe.

In one of the more illuminating works concerning the effects of our digital devices on our ability to focus and attend, *The Shallows: What the Internet Is Doing to Our Brains*, Nicholas Carr makes the point that the Internet and digital technologies are changing not just what we think but also the very process of thought itself, chipping away at our concentration and contemplation by presenting information to us in what he refers to as a swiftly moving stream of particles, those which by their very nature break our concentration into bits of unrelated knowledge.

As we jump from link to link on the Internet, or back and forth between text messages and a piece of virtual writing that we're attempting to apprehend, our awareness is rapidly being habituated toward a permanent state of distraction in which the former steady flow of our conscious mind is being incessantly interrupted in a manner that makes it increasingly impossible for us to fully focus our concentration or properly maintain our attention span.

As a result, we're increasingly losing the capacity to sink fully into a piece of writing or even our own stream of thoughts, much as a deep-sea diver would. Instead, according to Carr, as our capacity to attend grows more diffuse and distracted, we're increasingly losing the capacity to follow our stream of thoughts to a place of real depth, or to attend to a lengthy piece of writing in a manner that might allow us to sink fully into the author's point of view. Consequently, our intelligence may be growing narrower and less re-flective.

In his now famous article published in *The Atlantic*, "Is Google Making Us Stupid?" Carr makes mention of a research study undertaken by scholars at University College in London in which they examined the computer logs of visitors to two popular research sites. What they found was that people using the sites exhibited "a form of skimming activity," hopping from one source to another and rarely returning to any source they had already visited.

They typically read no more than one or two pages of an article before they "bounced" to another one. From this the researchers concluded that a new form of reading is emerging as users "power browse" through titles and contents in order to avoid reading in the traditional sense.

Increasingly, this is what appears to be the new default mechanism for many of us while reading online. As Maryanne Wolf, a developmental psychologist at Tufts University and author of *Proust and the Squid: The Story and Science of the Reading Brain*, puts it, the style of reading promoted by the Net, that in which we're endlessly bombarded by isolated bits of information and knowledge, may be weakening our capacity for the sort of deep reading that we need in order to apprehend complex works in the manner in which we formerly did.

When we read online, Wolf says, we tend to become only decoders of information, meaning that our ability to interpret what we are reading be-cause we are making important mental connections is being swallowed by our distracted minds.

Carr also goes on to make the point that the very algorithms by which we search for information on the World Wide Web by using powerful search engines like Google are likewise creating a disrupted awareness in many of us for the purpose of selling us more advertising. That is, the more pages we view by clicking on links, the greater opportunity these companies have to sell us more advertising even as our awareness becomes more interrupted and diffuse.

In a certain sense, one might say that the algorithms by which we search the Web and our own mental processes are increasingly becoming one and the same within a highly manipulative relationship in which we are being conditioned to attend to increasingly shorter bits of information and knowledge.

The point is that the Internet and digital technologies, as many people have already discovered through their own experience, are having certain adverse effects on our capacities for sustained concentration and deep reflection, with the real question looming on the horizon being one of asking if these effects are merely psychological in nature or are they in fact also physiological, and thus more permanent. Furthermore, as cognitive theorists and medical researchers are learning just how malleable and shaped by our psychological environment our brains really are, the question would appear to grow increasingly more prescient.

As such research continues, it remains to be seen how many of the adverse effects on the brain that digital technologies are engendering are indeed reversible, and how many are permanent. Yet if the latter is indeed the case, it would appear to be increasingly important that the modern world come to grips with just how the Internet and digital world may be significantly affecting our minds and brains at a level that is both long lasting and dangerous.

Particularly significant is the issue of how our working or short-term memory transfers information to our long-term memory, where it can be stored and used for us to think logically about the events of our lives, our selves, and about the world of which we are a part. Although our long-term memory has a nearly unlimited capacity, our short-term memory has only a limited amount of storage capacity. This means that as we're bombarded with increasingly more information in the virtual world, we're less able to store it in our working memory.

According to Tony Schwartz, productivity expert and author of *The Way We're Working Isn't Working*, when the working memory is experiencing information overload from the digital world,

> It's like having water poured into a glass continuously all day long, so that whatever was there at the top has to spill out as the new water comes down. We're constantly losing the information that's just come in—we're constantly replacing it, and there's no place to hold what we've already gotten.

As a result, our short-term memories are increasingly less able to hold the flux of information we receive from our digital devices so that it can then be passed on to our long-term memory, where it can be stored and used to think intelligently. Consequently, because we're most likely less able to efficiently use our long-term memories, we're likewise less able to make sense of the flood of information that is endlessly coming at us, with this unhealthy cycle between short and long-term memory endlessly perpetuating itself.

In addition, because we know that our digital devices and search engines can easily remember a piece of information for us, we're in effect outsourcing our working memories to those devices. As a recent *Scientific American* article, "The Internet Has Become the External Hard Drive for Our Memories," puts it, the interpersonal, social aspects of remembering are being increasingly replaced by a plethora of new digital tools. For example, in order to remember something, rather than trying to retrieve it from their memory bank or asking a friend, most people now simply grab their smartphone. As a result, because the retrieval of information is becoming increasingly an activity that is external to our own personal working memories, those which need to be stimulated through consistent use or by our interpersonal relations with others, our memories grow less functional and less able to transfer information to our long-term memories.

In addition, as the article states, being online all the time changes the subjective sense of self as the borders between personal memories and information distributed on the Internet start to blur. And when we use our circle of friends and acquaintances to help us remember things, we free up mental resources that otherwise would have been used to only retrieve specific information. As a result, we're able to use the memory of the members of our social grouping in total to access knowledge and information at a level that is much broader and deeper.

Yet our tendency to distribute information through this interpersonal memory network of face-to-face interactions is unfortunately now disappearing as we habitually pick up our smartphone or access Google on our computer or tablet in order to retrieve information in isolation. Consequently, our remembered field of knowledge in any specific area is now narrowing at the same time in which facts, information, and knowledge are no longer being as effectively inscribed into our biological memory banks.

There's also the issue of the endless amount of multitasking in which people are now engaged on their virtual devices, and how an endlessly distracted awareness engendered by such activity makes it more difficult for the brain to form memories. As Zaldy S. Tan, director of the Memory Disorders Clinic at Beth Israel Deaconess Medical Center, puts it, attention is the key to forming strong, lasting memories. "When we're not paying good attention," she says, "the memories we form aren't very robust, and we have a problem retrieving the information later."

Recently, researchers at MIT identified a neural circuit that helps the brain create lasting memories, and in doing so they discovered that the circuit was found to work more effectively when the brain is actively paying direct, immediate attention to what it is looking at, something that would appear to be in direct contradiction with the nature of digital multitasking, in which we jump endlessly back and forth between two specific tasks. In the same vein, numerous studies have also found that when students multitask while doing schoolwork, they understand and retain less information.

Scientists at the Institut National et de la Recherche Medicale (INSERM) in Paris uncovered evidence recently that while the right and left sides of the brain's prefrontal cortex work together when focused on a single task, the two sides work independently of each other when people attempt to perform two tasks at once. This they discovered when they asked participants in a study to complete two tasks at the same time while undergoing functional magnetic resonance imaging. Later, when the scientists asked the participants to attempt a third task, they found that they regularly forgot one of the three tasks they were asked to perform.

Similarly, in a 2006 study, researcher Russell Poldrack and two colleagues at the University of Texas at Austin asked participants to engage in a learning activity on a computer while also carrying out a second test, counting musical tones that sounded while they worked. Subjects who performed both tasks simultaneously initially appeared to learn just as well as subjects who did the first task only by itself. But upon further study, the researchers found that the former group was less able to extend and extrapolate their new knowledge to novel situations.

In addition, brain scans taken during the experiments revealed that different regions of the brain were active under the two conditions, indicating that the brain engages in a different form of memory when forced to pay attention to two streams of information at once. This suggests, the researchers concluded, "that even if distraction does not decrease the overall level of learning, it can result in the acquisition of knowledge that can be applied less flexibly in new situations."

If it is indeed the case that the two sides of our brain in fact work independently of each other when focusing on two things at once, and that leaves us less prepared to not only take in and absorb further information but actually use it creatively, it would seem that this might have profound implications for both our working memories and our creative thought processes as we attempt to effectively absorb information in a world where so many people are multitasking on various digital devices.

There's also the issue of the actual meaning our short-term memories may have for us as we attempt to incorporate them into a larger, long-term worldview, and the inherent danger of having this process interrupted. Harvard professor John Huth wrote recently in the *New York Times* of how when we "atomize knowledge into pieces that don't have a home in a larger conceptual framework," we tend to lose its meaning; consequently, it has less personal value for us. As a result, we become increasingly separated from what our personal experience in relation to the real, rather than the virtual, world might teach us.

One thinks immediately of all the unrelated bits of information one continually accesses online, those which often have very little (if any) relationship to one another, or else are provided to us with little or no context in which to place them. Consequently, as we become ever more habituated to taking in isolated pieces of information without making the effort to connect them to one another, or even have the time to do so simply because they are coming at us so quickly, our minds may easily grow less able to make such connections within the neurons and synapses of our physiological brains.

Consequently, as the isolated pieces of information relentlessly coming at us on our digital devices in what Carr describes as a swiftly moving stream of particles break the knowledge they might represent into atomized pieces, and as we grow less willing and able to unify those bits of information into something larger, it is easy to see how such larger knowledge that those bits of information are a part of could become increasingly inaccessible to us.

If it is indeed the case that our short-term memories are vanishing more quickly than they did before due to digital overload, and that consequently we're becoming less able to turn them into effective long-term memories, then it seems rather obvious that eventually this development is going to negatively affect people's capacity to develop a larger, more significant worldview, as well as our ability to examine that larger worldview in relation to our own lives, something that could easily affect someone searching for a larger, more expansive consciousness (a subject that will be taken up later in this work).

Neuroscientist Susan Greenfield, author of *Mind Change: How Digital Technologies Are Leaving Their Mark on Our Brains*, makes the argument that because our brains will adapt to whatever environment in which they're placed, and because our current cyber world is offering a new type of environment, our physiological brains could be changing in parallel, corresponding new ways. According to Greenfield, the human brain, that most sensitive of organs, is under attack, and we must wake up to the damage that our gadget-filled world may be doing to it.

Writing of how the actual neuronal networking in our entirely malleable brains can be easily affected by the bombardment of audiovisual stimuli that one encounters on one's digital or gaming devices, Greenfield goes on to say that while processing information is simply an appropriate response to an incoming stimuli, *understanding* requires that those stimuli be embedded in the sort of conceptual framework that is the result of connections between brain cells that occur as the consequence of one's experiences.

If the connections in our brains aren't being given enough time to develop as we move quickly from one bit of information to another on our digital devices, then the space in our minds needed for fully understanding our experiences could easily grow more limited. In fact, this would appear to be the very same dynamic that takes place when our short-term memories become overwhelmed to the point that they can't turn information and knowledge into long-term memories.

So if it is in fact the case that a distracted attention engendered in people by the Internet, and by their use of digital devices, is having a direct effect on their capacity to take in information, to turn short-term into long-term memories, and on the space that might develop inside our minds as we attempt to relate relevant information, then we may unfortunately be looking at some type of unhealthy, unbreakable chain, one that might be dumbing us all down in ways of which we're not even aware.

Chapter Three

Habituated to Addiction

Unfortunately, there is increasing evidence that people's need to continually surf the Web, multitask, send endless text messages, and so on, may be the result of an unhealthy physiological craving for the neurotransmitter dopamine. In her book *Find Your Focus Zone*, Lucy Palladino, the award-winning clinical psychologist, researcher, and author, writes of how when one is watching TV, playing video games, or otherwise involved with one's digital devices in an addictive manner, those things activate the basal ganglia of the brain, which release dopamine.

And when those dopamine levels in your brain increase, you're inclined to do whatever it takes to maintain the "high" that comes from the sense of well-being that results, but when the levels decrease, one inevitably starts looking for some distraction to replace that chemical happiness.

In similar fashion, a 2014 article by Pauline Anderson in *Medscape*, in reporting news from the American Psychiatric Association's 2014 annual meeting, made mention of how Internet addiction can be linked to dopamine changes in the brain, the article indicating that prolonged Internet use leads to a reduction in the brain's dopamine transporters. As a result, the excess of dopamine that subsequently builds up in the brain's neurons results in a type of euphoria that can lead to addictive behavior.

Another 2012 article in *The Atlantic*, "Exploiting the Neuroscience of Internet Addiction," by Bill Davidow, warned that what we do online can release dopamine into the brain's pleasure centers, resulting in obsessive pleasure-seeking behavior, and of how technology companies are able to exploit this form of addiction for profit.

Warning of how people can become trapped in a dopamine compulsion loop as the neurons in the brain that release the neurotransmitter grow excited as people compulsively check their email or obsessively post on Facebook or Twitter, the article refers to how Internet companies are learning how to specifically use this new form of obsession to increase their profits.

In quoting Thomas Edison as saying, "I find out what the world needs. Then I go ahead and invent it," the article goes on to discuss how since the advent of Web 2.0, the key to success for digital companies has been creating obsessions. In fact, Internet gaming companies are now openly discussing compulsion loops that directly result in obsessions, while the goal of other digital applications is the same: to create the compulsion to gather as many friends on Facebook or followers on Twitter as possible, or to be pleasantly surprised to find on Foursquare that a friend you haven't seen for years lives nearby.

In a 2014 article by Jeanene Swanson, "The Neurological Basis for Digital Addiction," Dr. David Greenfield, a pioneer in the field of virtual addiction and founder of the Center for Internet Technology Addiction in Connecticut, is quoted as describing Internet addiction as a digital drug operating on what he calls a form of *variable-ratio reinforcement*, meaning that when you never know what you're going to get next, such as what occurs when one is checking their email or text messages, or looking for "likes" on their Facebook or Twitter page, and that person has a compulsive need to find out, dopamine circuits are activated, and a small surge is released into the brain, people then becoming addicted to what he terms the *dopaminergic hit*.

New York Times bestselling author and neuroscientist Daniel J. Levitin, founding dean of arts and humanities at the Minerva Schools at Keck Graduate Institute in California, taking on the subject of multitasking in his book, *The Organized Mind*, writes of how multitasking on digital technologies creates a dopamine-addiction feedback look, effectively rewarding the brain for losing focus and for constantly searching for external stimulation.

If it is indeed true that people's Internet addictions may in fact be filling their physiological brains with dopamine through their endless use of social media sites, or the need to continually surf the Web or send text messages, then this behavior might indeed have a certain unhealthy chemical basis. And if people's need to jump from place to place on their digital devices is a result of this sort of chemical dependency, then there might indeed be an unhealthy link between the distracted awareness that our Internet age is engendering in people and their subservience to their own physiological impulses.

In *The Shallows*, Nicholas Carr writes that if you wanted to invent the perfect medium that would rewire our brain circuits to result in this type of obsessive behavior, you couldn't do any better than the Internet. That is to say, the Internet delivers the exact type of sensory and cognitive stimuli—intensive, interactive, addictive—that have been shown to result in strong and rapid alterations in brain function. Add to Carr's conjecture the sort of obsessive-compulsive dopamine loop that might affect one's brain chemistry, and you have the perfect mechanism for digital companies to keep people addicted to their products by how they are using them.

Internet addiction may also significantly limit the free flow of information on the Internet with others as those who are looking for their next "fix" by obsessively posting on Facebook or Twitter will look only for information that confirms their particular worldview because they can retrieve it much more quickly than knowledge or information that inhabits a gray area where the truth is not always so clear. So, rather than go through the throes of withdrawal, they tend to look only for those items to post that are consistent with their own opinion on certain subject matters.

In addition, as people become more addicted to the need to carve out a particular identity for themselves in cyberspace by posting certain items or hitting the "like" button for other people's posts or tweets that confirm that particular identity, even though it might not be one that represents their true self in real time and space, our honest sharing of information with each other could be inhibited even further.

According to Susan Greenfield, an identity on Facebook is implicit rather than explicit, meaning that users show rather than tell by stressing their likes and dislikes instead of elaborating on their actual life narrative. When such is the case, it seems more than obvious how easy it might be to create a false narrative about oneself that is being presented to others.

In addition, says Greenfield in *Mind Change*, those who tend to use Facebook to create this somewhat illusory narrative about themselves are likewise those who are most dependent on the site for self-expression, even though that self-expression to others may paradoxically be artificial and limited.

What seems so dangerous about this is simply how easy it has become to create an alternative narrative about oneself by simply pressing the "like" button on our Facebook page, or typing opinions about various issues within the 280-character parameters of Twitter, instead of having face-to-face conversations with other people that include all of the complex interpersonal dynamics which might be involved.

Therefore, one can see how easy it has become to create such an illusory narrative to which other people respond with their own illusory narratives; this circular process then continues until eventually one may be operating, at least in the virtual world, through some sort of false, disembodied self.

If it is indeed true that many people are using social media sites to create illusory identities, then it seems possible that this development might have actual ramifications for people's emotive and mental health. The radical psychiatrist from the 1960s and 1970s, R. D. Laing, in his pioneering book about madness, *The Divided Self*, wrote of how people who are growing schizoid or even schizophrenic create a false self that they present to others in order to protect their true selves from being engulfed by the world. Then, as they continue to relate to others increasingly through this false self, the true self inside them grows dead and disembodied as its contacts with the world and others grow increasingly unreal.

What Laing, who has now passed away, would say to others about the effects of our Internet age on our identities and mental health is now only conjecture. Yet one imagines he might be more than a little concerned with how people relate increasingly to others in cyberspace in a manner in which it has become all too easy to create an illusory self or false identity.

The danger that Internet addiction in cyberspace, along with the obsessive need to cultivate an alternative, more attractive personality on social media, presents is that these activities may well lead toward information sharing with others that reinforces one's addiction simply because both of these compulsions are a function of seeking only that knowledge or those facts that will either provide an immediate fix or reinforce the self that one is attempting to present to others on the Web. Therefore, as the information that one is drawn to in the digital world grows narrower and more exclusive, the strength of one's addiction grows with it.

That is, as the information that one seeks has an increasingly narrow focus, the addictive knot is pulled ever tighter as the range in which one looks for pertinent facts or knowledge to confirm his previous postings grows more constricted, leading toward one's addictive impulses growing increasingly intense.

If someone has obsessively posted information on Facebook or Twitter in reference to a particular political or social argument, then it may be the case that to keep one's Internet addiction intact, or to keep substantiating the particular identity that one has been presenting to others, one begins to scavenge only for information or knowledge that is consistent with the specific worldview that he or she has adopted.

At the same time, there is in fact increasing evidence of a connection between dopamine and obsessive-compulsive disorder (OCD) as scientists discover that dopamine levels are higher in those who suffer from it.

OCD, as John Aubri, contributing researcher and writer to *Livestrong*, writes about in his 2015 article, is characterized by obsessive thought patterns brought on by extreme anxiety, with these thoughts then driving individuals to somehow bring them to fruition by completing the tasks they obsess about. In many cases, people succumb to certain rituals or tasks that they feel they must perform in order for something catastrophic not to happen to them. Engaging in these rituals results in a sort of relief from their anxiety that can also bring a sense of pleasure.

In addition, if one looks at the type of obsessive posting that many people now do on social media, it seems reasonable to classify this type of Internet addiction as a form of OCD, something that many mental health professionals are currently doing.

In a 2015 study undertaken by researchers in India in order to study the potential relationship between Internet addiction and obsessive-compulsive disorder, and published in *Innovations in Clinical Neuroscience*, the researchers concluded in their study that a greater number of OCD subjects exhibited Internet addiction symptoms than did the control subjects who were part of the study. Furthermore, the researchers concluded that higher rates of OCD existed in those who could be said to manifest Internet addiction.

Recently, scientists have begun researching the role that dopamine plays in OCD. Using PET scans and other types of imaging, researchers have discovered that there is in fact an overproduction of dopamine in individuals with OCD. In one 2003 study, whose results were published in the *European Journal of Nuclear Medicine and Molecular Imaging*, the dopamine transporter density of fifteen OCD subjects was compared with that of nineteen neurotypical subjects. Results showed that dopamine levels were higher in the OCD subjects, leading the researchers to conclude that dopamine plays a direct role in the pathophysiology of OCD.

Certain parts of the brain, mainly the basal ganglia and the frontal cortex, work together to guide behavior. When there is too much activity in the basal ganglia area, an overproduction of dopamine occurs. Referring to this overproduction of the neurotransmitter, Bill Harris, director of the Centerpointe Research Institute in Beaverton, Oregon, a facility that assists people in eliminating the stress from their life by engaging in deep meditation techniques and other such practices, said recently that another part of the brain affected by this overproduction of dopamine is the cingulate gyrus.

This area, says Harris, "has a lot to do with a person's ability to shift attention, be cognitively flexible, adapt to circumstances, to move easily from one idea to another, to 'go with the flow,' and to be cooperative."

Of course, physical subservience to a dopamine loop and a compulsive need to present an alternative identity to others on social media are just two of the digital addictions to which many people might be succumbing. In fact, there is now an actual name for Internet addiction—Internet Use Disorder (IUD)—that includes a range of symptoms. According to Hilarie Cash, PhD, cofounder of the Restart Internet Addiction Recovery Program, these symptoms are a compulsive checking of text messages; frequent changing of Facebook status and uploading of "selfies"; a feeling of euphoria while on the Web; social withdrawal; loss of interest in activities that don't involve a computer, phone, or gadget; and feelings of restlessness when one is unable to go online.

Many of these symptoms would appear to be part of a paradoxical dynamic about which Sherry Turkle, professor of the social studies of science and technology at MIT and author of the book *Alone Together*, has written. In writing about how the more digitally connected a person is, the more alone they tend to feel, Turkle attributes this phenomenon to the fact that when one is constantly connected to the digital world on the Internet, the more of a commodity that person can become, someone who can easily compare him- or herself to others and be found wanting.

Turkle's book is the result of her fifteen-year exploration of our lives in the digital world. Based on interviews with hundreds of children and adults, it describes new, unsettling relationships between friends, lovers, parents, and community, as well as the dynamics of intimacy and solitude in our new Internet age.

According to Turkle, technology has become the architect of our intimacies. Drawn by the illusion of companionship without the demands of intimacy, we engage in "risk free" relationships and connections in the digital world, and in so doing confuse the scattershot postings on a Facebook wall or responses on Twitter with authentic communication. In the process, we become less connected with people and more connected to simulations of them.

Turkle's book goes on to say that while Internet technologies allow us to do everything everywhere, we begin to eventually feel overwhelmed and depleted by the lives that technology makes possible. We may be free to take our smartphones and tablets with us and in so doing work anywhere, but we are also prone to being lonely everywhere. In a surprising, ironical way, constant connection leads toward a new loneliness. We turn to technology to fill the void, but as technology ramps up, our emotional lives ramp down.

The danger here, relative to Internet addiction, is that as one begins to feel more isolated in the digital world, one grows increasingly compelled to establish more fulfilling connections within it until one's addictions are at last dictating one's behavior—or at least until one engages in an endless search for greater connection within the virtual world that one is likely never going to find.

Then, as one grows more addicted to the use of one's digital devices, the more distracted one's attention becomes as their short-term memory is increasingly flooded with a plethora of knowledge and information that it becomes impossible to absorb. Eventually, the storage capacity of one's long-term memory is affected by one's depleted short-term memory. Over time, this becomes a self-perpetuating cycle as one greedily searches in vain for the information and knowledge that will allow one's clarity of mind and ability to attend to return to their natural states of equilibrium.

If it is true that people in our current digital age are becoming lost in a land of distracted awareness in which both their short- and long-term memories are being compromised, fueled by potentially unhealthy chemical dependencies originating within their own bodies, and an increasing need to escape their true selves by presenting an idealized self to the virtual world, then it may not just be our capacity to remember, learn, and think creatively that may be compromised. It may likewise be our capacity to potentially achieve an expanded consciousness concerning ourselves and our world that is in serious jeopardy as people become increasingly conditioned, both physically and psychologically, to engage their world with a less focused, less insightful awareness, one that was prevalent before the advent of an Internet age that began causing that awareness to fragment due to the information and knowledge that people have begun receiving in increasingly smaller, fragmented pieces.

Yet before we can look at how this search for an expansive intelligence might be affected by what the Internet might be doing to our minds and physiological brains, it seems important to look at the effects that various forms of digital addiction and the ways we're using our digital devices might be having on memory and attention. Without a healthy working memory and a focused ability to attend, the search for a larger awareness, one that begins with an examination of the structure of our thinking minds, becomes impossible to pursue.

In addition, what needs to be studied is exactly how the capacity to attend is being affected in those who use their digital devices in addictive ways or in those who are determined to be suffering from Internet addiction. As many neuroscientists and cognitive theorists already know, because our attention spans are dependent upon our working memory, when our working memories are overtaxed with too much information, our brains become overtaxed and, consequently, easily distracted.

In addition, recent experiments indicate that as we reach the limits of our working memory, it becomes harder to distinguish relevant from irrelevant information. And when it becomes harder to separate information and knowledge that is significant to what one is attempting to comprehend from that which is insignificant, it becomes much more difficult to attend to the area under scrutiny as further information is soon lost under a fog of irrelevancy.

John Sweller is an Australian educational psychologist who has spent three decades studying how our minds process information, and how we learn. His cognitive load theory suggests that effective learning in any subject area can only be facilitated when one's cognitive resources are directed toward information and knowledge that is relevant to that learning, meaning that irrelevant information that is not directly related to whatever one is endeavoring to learn will lead toward a cognitive overload that makes it very difficult, if not impossible, to integrate into one's working memory whatever one is attempting to grasp.

Sweller found in one of his studies undertaken to study cognitive overload that when learners were provided with too much irrelevant information, they were able to solve certain problems they were asked to solve relative to the knowledge they were endeavoring to acquire, but, at the same time, they remained oblivious to the essential structure of the problem area with which they had become acquainted. In fact, Sweller goes on to point to experiments demonstrating that this type of conventional problem solving in which learners are not able to grasp the actual structure of what they are learning can have negative consequences for that learning.

Comprehending the actual structure of a subject area that one is endeavoring to grasp, whether as a student, a lay person, a professional, or someone simply attempting to examine his or her world, is critical to fully internalizing that subject area in addition to being critical for the development of long-term memory and attention. And as will be dealt with later in this work, the ability to fully internalize a structure is critical to examining the structure of both one's thinking mind and one's self.

What exactly is the relationship between digital addiction, short- and long-term memory, attention, and our capacity to internalize and structure our world, our experiences, and even our own thought processes so that we can learn from them? To answer that question, we need to briefly consider how the spatial map in the hippocampus region of our brains aids in this process.

The spatial map, which is essentially an internal representation of our external environment, aids us in focusing our attention on the details of our world by allowing us to formulate an internalized picture of it. It's also a type of cognitive map that allows us to not only create long-term memories but also have access to them later.

Without this sort of internal reference point, we could easily end up as Jean-Paul Sartre's anti-hero Antoine Roquentin in the famous existential novel *Nausea*, someone who reaches the point in his iconic, vivid encounter with a chestnut tree where he suddenly loses all ability to abstract or conceptualize his world, and so is left with the naked terror inherent in pure existence. In other words, without this cognitive mapping our capacity for focused attention would soon disappear simply because we would be unable to conceptualize what our experiences are telling us in order that we might put them into a clear perspective.

Our explicit memories, those that require conscious recall, as opposed to implicit memories (which are habitual, unconscious, and automatic), require a degree of selective attention for that recall to occur. As much as anything, attention acts as a conscious filter in this process in order to prevent us from becoming overwhelmed by a flood of information and perceptions that we couldn't possibly simultaneously internalize.

When our short-term memories become overwhelmed by too much information to the point that they can't effectively create long-term memories, our ability to attend suffers, as does our capacity to internalize our world through the cognitive mapping that is vital to this internalization process. At the same time, as our capacity to conceptualize our world suffers, so does our ability to hold the world at bay, so to speak, as we try to make sense of it. Ultimately, as this inhibiting process continues, we're less able to learn whatever lessons our environment and other people may be subtly teaching us through our own experience.

Selective attention is also what unifies our conscious experience. Aldous Huxley wrote of how the brain's capacity for processing sensory information is more limited than its ability to take in everything from its immediate environment. Attention acts as a filter, selecting some objects for further processing while discarding others in order to limit the amount of experiences with which our minds must deal. As a result, internal representations of our world do not represent every aspect of one's external world with which one is in contact as we focus on specific sensory information that may be useful to us while ignoring the rest.

In their book *The Distracted Mind*, in order to demonstrate the role of selective attention in the minds of our prehistoric ancestors, Adam Gazzaley, professor of neurology at the University of California, San Francisco, and Larry Rosen, professor of psychology at California State University, Dominguez Hills, use the example of one of our thirsty ancestors, prowling through a deep forest before emerging into an unfamiliar clearing, where he spots an enticing stream. As he does so, Gazzaley and Rosen recount how the prehistoric ancestor uses his selective attention to provide himself with multisensory information concerning the possible presence of a man-eating jaguar: listening for the deep guttural noise a jaguar makes while waiting and hiding in the bushes, directing his vision to watch for the jaguar's characteristic orange and black pattern, and directing his olfactory sense toward the possible presence of the animal's musky smell while also, knowing that the jaguar tends to hunt on the left bank of a stream, directing his attention toward that same part of the bushes lining the water.

In other words, this is an example of selective attention converging across several different sensory areas in pursuit of the goal of determining whether a man-eating animal lurks in the bushes, hoping to make a tasty meal of the prehistoric man. At the same time that he is employing his capacity for selective attention, the ancestor is likewise choosing to discard other dynamics that are extraneous to his purpose of keeping himself safe, such as a bird emerging abruptly from the thicket, a wind blowing suddenly through the trees, or even various shadows being made by the sun passing overhead in the pool of water.

At the same time, long-term memory certainly has a significant role to play in selective attention, serving as a bridge between perceptions and future actions. That is, if our prehistoric man had not been able to use his working memory, one solidified through experience as short-term memories were effectively turned into long-term ones, he would have had no idea what aspects of his immediate environment should have commanded his attention in safeguarding himself from a hungry animal. In addition, the ancestor's interior cognitive mapping of a familiar environment plays a significant role in assisting him toward where he should direct his attention.

Short-term memories turned into long-term ones, the formation of a spatial map in the brain's hippocampus region as the result of long-term memory, and the selective attention that is a significant product of this cognitive mapping—this entire process is what allows us to be the sort of intelligent creatures who can learn from our world and from our immediate environment, each of these dynamics being significantly dependent upon the one preceding it.

Yet if this entire process is short-circuited at the beginning by such things as a distracted attention, or by the cognitive overload that results when too much information is coming at someone too quickly, potentially fueled by unhealthy chemical addictions, then the other mental processes that normally follow might likewise be negatively affected.

Short-term memories will be impeded from becoming long-term ones. As a result, a clear spatial mapping of one's environment will have a lesser chance of being effectively internalized. Then, without such a clear internalization, it becomes more difficult to selectively attend to important elements of one's world while blocking out irrelevant ones. Ultimately, our capacity to learn is affected when we can no longer focus clearly on the information and knowledge that is important for us to absorb.

What happens when the brain loses its ability to selectively filter information? What exactly are the long-term consequences for our thinking minds, and for the concurrent growth of our intelligence? To discover the answer to these questions, we really need to begin looking at the processes of thought and memory, how they operate and what specifically are their limitations.

Chapter Four

Thought, Memory, and Reality

We take both thought and memory for granted. That is, we believe that we can grasp the particulars of our world by thinking logically about them and likewise assume that our memories pertain to events and circumstances in our lives that by and large occurred the way we remember them. In other words, the reality of both processes is rarely, if ever, questioned.

Yet some who have thought deeply about this matter, those who have done so by being able to at least temporarily step outside the structure of thought and the nature of memory, have found that both processes not only have their own unique limitations but also are not as real as most people have always taken them to be.

However, undertaking such an intrinsic examination of our thinking mind in relation to our external reality, and carefully examining memory in relation to the nature of time and the past, means having the sort of clear-sighted apprehension that can only be called into service when one's ability to attend, to formulate a clear internalized picture of one's world, and to access one's long-term memories are all processes that are operating optimally.

Any number of psychologists, philosophers, and thinkers have written about how our memories of past events in our lives are essentially products of our thinking minds that can never re-create past events and circumstances exactly as they occurred, or as we experienced them at the time, meaning that we're forever creating in our minds a past that isn't entirely real. Some, such as the late philosopher-thinker Jiddu Krishnamurti, have even gone so far as to suggest that all knowledge, because it is a product of the past, needs to be looked at with the same suspicious eye.

During a series of conversations that Krishnamurti had over the years with the famous twentieth-century physicist David Bohm, the two of them often discussed the nature of knowledge in relation to thought, the past, and memory. Bohm had originally become interested in the philosophy of Krishnamurti upon hearing of Krishnamurti's contention that the observer is the observed.

As a quantum physicist, Bohm had been deeply immersed in the dynamics of the quantum world, that in which since the time of Werner Heisenberg physicists have maintained that the observer of quantum reality at the level of the very small can't help but affect that reality merely by the process of observing it. So Bohm had been immediately struck by Krishnamurti's contention.

The two men often discussed the process of image-making in the mind in relation to how images of our world that we create prevent us from experiencing the world and ourselves as they really are. In relation to this idea, they spoke often of whether the movement of thought, which creates the past and memory, could ever come to a complete stop so that we might discover whether some larger reality beyond rational thought actually exists.

Both men have since passed on. Krishnamurti died in 1986 at the age of ninety, and David Bohm died in 1992 at the age of seventy-four. Yet their fascinating dialogues have been preserved in a number of publications and videotapes.

What remains from their discussions is the far-reaching idea that the process of thought might have distinct limitations in terms of how our thinking minds create an illusory conception of our world, the past, and even knowledge itself. Likewise, once again, there is the idea that a clearer perception of our world and ourselves in search of a larger awareness might necessitate discovering exactly how the movement of thought might come to an end within each of us.

The revered ancient Chinese philosopher Lao Tzu referred to a similar state of clarity in which thought might come to an end and everything is fulfilled in his iconic book *Tao Te Ching* when he wrote, "If you realize that you have enough / you are truly rich. / If you stay in the center / and embrace death with your whole heart / you will endure forever."

The remarkable implication of what these men meant by their seemingly confounding, yet potentially illuminating, statements is something that most likely can only be fleshed out if one is able to at least temporarily step outside his or her thinking mind to examine, at a deeply intuitive level, their true meaning. More than anything, the reality to which Krishnamurti and Lao Tzu point almost certainly has to do with the illusory nature of thought and memory—things that might prevent us from being in touch with a larger intelligence that may lie beyond them.

Yet if in this new digital age the capacity of our brain to turn short-term into long-term memories, our ability to focus and attend, and our capability to create a clear, internal picture of the particulars of our world are being threatened by how we are using our digital devices, then this situation may indeed have profound implications for the sort of search for a larger awareness about which Krishnamurti and Bohm often spoke.

More than anything, as we continue to increasingly outsource our memories to Google or other search engines and memory devices such as Echo, compromise our capacity to attend by facilitating a distracted awareness, and subject ourselves to more knowledge and information than our working memories can possibly absorb through our online addictions, we may eventually find ourselves in serious danger of losing the subtlety of mind necessary to examine our thinking minds in search of something larger.

What's more, it is easy to see how this loss of mental acuity can easily become institutionalized over the coming decades as our digital world begins to slowly but surely take over everything: our commerce, our personal relations, our patterns of learning, and how we acquire information and knowledge. Eventually, there might not be people like Krishnamurti or David Bohm in the world simply because people will have lost the mental capacity to discover what Krishnamurti had discovered, and what he and David Bohm had spent time discussing.

What will almost certainly be lost is the realization of how time changes memory until, as Marcel Proust alluded to in his iconic work *In Search of Lost Time (Remembrance of Things Past)*, people will lose the apprehension of how the past is always elusive, and the act of remembering something perfectly is a labor in vain.

After his years as a young man came instantly back to him with a seemingly stark clarity after he swallowed a madeleine cookie, and its taste immediately connected him to a flood of memories, Proust continued to write of his experiences of this time in his life. Yet, as he did so, he came to the realization that in the act of remembering his past, he was always changing it, and so made endless revisions to his manuscript, right up to the moment of his death.

Neuroscientists have known for decades now that memories exist as subtle shifts in the strength of synaptic connections between the brain's neurons. As cells become intertwined in the brain's neuronal structure, new memories are made. Yet, as those new memories of the same situations or experiences continue to be made, the original memories are altered to the point that they actually cease to exist. So each time we remember something, we are moving further away from our original remembrance of it.

According to Jonah Lehrer, author of the immensely popular book *Proust Was a Neuroscientist*, a series of experiments was conducted at New York University in 2000 in which the scientists who conducted experiments with a group of rats discovered that the act of remembering something, every time it took place, diminished how accurately the rats remembered it. They demonstrated this fact by successfully blocking long-term remembrance of a painful shock to which the rats had been subjected by interrupting the process of how the rats remembered the memory. What they found was that the rats' long-term remembrance of the painful shock was not only altered but in fact disappeared completely, to the point that the rats actually became, as Lehrer puts it, amnesiac to the entire process.

If it is indeed true that each time we remember something, the memory of that event becomes less accurate, then that would appear to be powerful evidence of how our remembrance of the past, and the knowledge that might emanate from it, may often be illusory products of our thinking minds, something Krishnamurti devoted his life to trying to make clear to others.

Yet how could those of us who are interested in exploring the structure of our thinking minds, knowledge, and the past in search of a larger consciousness do this if our working memories, our attention spans, and our capacity to internalize the world in which we exist are not left intact in the midst of this new digital age we have entered, one in which all of the above may well be under assault? The answer would appear to be that we couldn't, due to a number of different factors.

First of all, if people's capacity to effectively turn short-term recollections into long-term memories is so compromised by the glut of information from the digital world that it becomes increasingly difficult to absorb that information, or if their capacity to attend is compromised by that same information overload, people may easily over time lose the capacity to examine the nature of memory itself simply through having lost their once clear access to it.

Then, over time, as it becomes increasingly difficult to step outside memory and the past in order to carefully scrutinize them simply because memory's relation to the past has grown foggier, it seems inevitable that it will become ever more difficult for people to come to the realization of how memory, the past, and the structure of thought itself are inextricably connected. Eventually, as the digital world increasingly leaves its mark on people's thinking minds and physiological brains, this search for the exact nature of the relationship between thought, the past, memory, and knowledge might over time become a genuine impossibility.

In addition, as people's short-term memories, and consequently their attention spans become ever more diluted by the amount of facts and information coming at them on their digital devices, their capacity for lengthy introspective thought might be similarly compromised as their thinking minds begin to lose the capacity for the sort of uninterrupted, long-term attention span that is able to follow a single thought all the way to its original source.

If people are living with an increasingly distracted attention due to information overload, and if their internal cognitive map has grown fuzzier due to their increasing inability to turn short-term recollections into long-term memories, then it seems inevitable that a potential search for the exact nature of the relationship between thought, memory, the past, and knowledge will become one that becomes increasingly impossible to undertake.

The great existential philosophers such as John-Paul Sartre and Albert Camus examined in their work a *nothingness*, a void that they postulated was the very ground of our existence, one in which we create the *being* in which we live through our thinking minds. Sartre confronted this nothingness in *Nausea* through his main character's incapacity to keep what Sartre saw as the naked terror of pure existence at bay by losing his ability to conceptualize the particulars of his world through his thinking mind. A neuroscientist might say he had lost the complete use of his internal, cognitive map.

Camus, in his great novel *The Stranger*, writes of the anti-hero Mersault, who shoots a strange man on the beach simply to assert the possibility of the terrible freedom that he realizes we all possess, and then spends time waiting in his prison cell to be executed, much as many of us wait in our own existential prison cells as we attempt to come to grips with the potential absurdity of our existence.

To be sure, many other great existential philosophers and writers (Heidegger, Dostoevsky, Husserl, Kafka) were brave enough to confront the nothingness that is at the core of our being, and most did brilliantly. Yet, at the same time, it seems that perhaps they didn't go far enough in their search. If they did, they might have somehow come out the other side, as did those such as Aldous Huxley, even if only temporarily, in his experiences with the drug mescaline, and in so doing discovering that to which Lao Tzu alluded when he wrote, "The Tao is like a well: / used but never used up. / It is like the eternal void / filled with infinite possibilities."

In this iconic book, *The Doors of Perception*, Huxley recounts how after swallowing some mescaline he was transported into a world of pure existence similar to the one Sartre's Roquentin experienced throughout *Nausea*, but particularly during his encounter with the chestnut tree. Only the pure existence that Huxley discovered, rather than being terrifying and without meaning, was one of infinite wonder and beauty.

Flowers in a vase shone with a stunning inner light. Four bamboo chair legs, with their intricate beauty, brought Huxley immediate insight into the very nature of things. The stoical serenity inherent in some window drapes revealed them as not just another household item but also a true silken wilderness. Indeed, Huxley was able to experience Eternity in a flower, Infinity in four chair legs, the Absolute in the folds in a pair of flannel trousers, and a blank stucco wall with a shadow slanting across it as being unforgettably beautiful—empty but charged with all the meaning and mystery of existence.

Granted, Huxley entered this new world of consciousness artificially through the use of a drug. Yet at the same time it still seems possible that those of us who are interested might find a way to enter such a world without the use of mescaline or some other consciousness-expanding drug and, in so doing, apprehending the beauty and mystery that might be available to us if only we could find a way to live in the world while also dispensing with the barrier of conceptual thought whenever it is not needed, that which often keeps us removed from a world of pure experience.

Yet if we are to begin the journey of stepping outside our thinking mind, and to observe the movement of thought from a quiet place outside it—a place that allows us to see how the movement of thought and the illusions of the past, memory, and the self might all emanate from the same source—it seems almost certain that it will be necessary to do so with an attention that is focused and undistracted, and with full access to our long-term memories so that we can in fact apprehend their potentially illusive nature.

Also extremely important in this quest is having full access to an internal, cognitive mapping of our environment and our experiences so that we can hold them at arm's length in order to examine how conditioned we all are by the world in which we live.

Obviously, if one agrees with what has been said previously in this work, these are all dynamics upon which our current digital age is having a seriously deleterious effect. That is, the idea that people today, with the distracted awareness that is being created in many of them by digital overload, and by their increasing need to jump endlessly between links, websites, and text messages, would have the necessary inner discipline and attention span to follow a single thought to its purest source would appear at times to be an absurdity.

Likewise, the endeavor to examine, as Marcel Proust did, the illusory nature of memory when people's short-term memories are being filled with so much knowledge and information at such a rapid rate that it becomes increasingly difficult to convert those memories into long-term ones would appear to be likewise an often elusive search, one in which it becomes nearly impossible to comprehend exactly how new memories are constantly changing our view of the past, and of ourselves.

Also, if we are to examine our own conditioning until we reach the point that we realize exactly how conditioned we are by the world in which we live, and if we are to ever free ourselves from that conditioning in search of some larger awareness, it seems inevitable that we must first have full access to the internal representation of our world that exists within ourselves, one that necessitates a fully focused attention and clear access to our memories of past experiences.

In short, in order to examine our thinking minds in search of a larger intelligence means that we necessarily must have unfettered, clear access to our thoughts and memories so that we might be able to carefully examine them in order to see exactly where they might lead.

As many who came of age during the time when the writings of Huxley fueled the popular imagination might remember, Carlos Castaneda wrote a series of books recounting his experiences with the Yaqui Indian Don Juan. In them, Don Juan serves as a mentor of sorts, attempting to instruct Castaneda in how to become what he refers to as *a man of knowledge*, someone who is able to put him or herself in touch with a reality that might exist on the other side of rational thought.

In a series of instructions recounted in the book *Tales of Power*, Don Juan speaks of the need to sweep or shrink what he refers to as the *tonal*, all of those things that are creations of the self, in order to approach what he calls the *nagual*, the realm of the limitless that exists apart from the world of mundane, two-dimensional reality—something that can only be grasped, as he tells Castaneda, through intuitive, direct insight.

Although the latter books in the series tend to be highly stylized and full of rituals that often seem at times as if they might in fact be somehow clouding the larger truth behind them, Don Juan's urging of Castaneda to step outside the self, one's thinking mind, one's conceptions of the world, and one's past in order to examine them in the search for a larger intelligence is very similar to what people such as Krishnamurti or David Bohm spent their lives encouraging others to do.

What Krishnamurti, David Bohm, or Carlos Castandeda would say about our current digital age if they were alive today is of course only conjecture. Yet one imagines that they might be troubled by what people's obsessive use of smartphones, tablets, Google, social media, and the Internet itself is doing to their clarity of mind, particularly the distracted attention and lack of clear access to memory in relation to the self and the past that are being imbued in so many by the digital overload being engendered by our current cyber world.

Of particular concern to them might be how Alan Watts's *stream of life*, something about which he wrote in his classic book *The Wisdom of Insecurity*—that timeless flow of events in our lives which we are forever impeding and cutting ourselves off from by our reliance on fixed concepts about our world—is being so consistently interrupted by people's need these days to jump endlessly between online postings or between social media and communication with others vis-à-vis text messaging or email.

Of further concern might be how people are so often creating fictitious selves in the cyber world before they have made the journey inside themselves to discover the nature of their true selves within real space and time.

Most people, of course, might never pursue a larger intelligence while they are alive in this world, being content to focus exclusively on their jobs, families, adventures, and the transitory pleasures of their lives. Yet for those rare people who might in fact do so, particularly those young people who have come of age exclusively as digital natives, it seems imperative that the potential damage done to the subtlety of their thinking minds by the digital world with all its devices be kept to a minimum if they are to have any chance at all in being successful with this otherworldly journey.

Chapter Five

A Distracted Awareness and the River of Thought

As Krishnamurti said many times, the movement of thought and time are one and the same. Using the analogy of a pendulum, he spoke of how our thinking minds are always swinging back and forth between past and future, a movement that excludes anything new simply because the future, as we envision it, is simply a projection of what has occurred to us in the past.

Consequently, he often asked the question of whether thought itself is ever capable of seeing anything new or of living entirely in the present. To do so, he often postulated the necessity of living in and extending that period of silence that takes place between two thoughts, and in doing so, discovering a certain state of being that liberates one from his or her conditioning while pointing toward something larger.

Yet it would appear to be rather obvious that the enemy of this attempt to live in that space between one's thoughts is the distracted awareness that is being engendered in so many people today through the use of their digital devices and the effect that the Internet is having upon all of us. As one jumps endlessly between webpages, social media posts, and email and text messages, it seems veritably impossible that one might be aware of the movement of thought within oneself. Rather, that movement is being externally controlled by the digital world in a manner that it most likely never has been before throughout the history of mankind.

In fact, it may well be this type of external control of our conscious attention by the Internet, or by how we use our smartphones, PCs, and tablets, that has now become a genuine enemy to not only our focused awareness but also our ability to think creatively. From how we have outsourced our working memories to Google to how the algorithms that emanate from powerful search engines habitually direct our attention, our thinking minds are in a very real sense becoming increasingly externalized to the point that we may be losing touch with how the process of thought itself operates.

Russell Poldrack's 2006 study, which determined that subjects who learn two tasks or bits of knowledge simultaneously often lose the capacity to extend new knowledge to novel situations, may well be the tip of the proverbial iceberg as far as our capacity to think creatively is concerned, conceivably demonstrating that distracted thought is the enemy of an expanded awareness. Almost certainly, it is the enemy of a quiet mind that might attempt to inhabit, even if only temporarily, the space between two thoughts.

It is also an obvious enemy of the stream of life to which Alan Watts often referred simply because of how when the conscious flow of our awareness is continually interrupted, as it is today in the digital world by scattered bits of knowledge and information, the awareness of that stream can easily disappear.

Adam Gazzaley and Larry D. Rosen, in their book *The Distracted Mind*, write about the issue of cognitive control, describing how the highly evolved goal-setting abilities that are inevitably part of multitasking activities often collide headfirst with fundamental limitations of our cognitive capacities and, in the process, create a distracted attention, meaning that when our attempt to focus on several things at once meets the limits of our own cognitive capabilities, our attention can become scattered and diffuse.

Of course, the fundamental question underlying this concern is one of asking whether our cognitive capacities can simultaneously grow and change in order to accommodate themselves to the new models for working and learning that are now taking place in our current digital age or whether we in fact possess inherent cognitive limitations that, when stretched too far in this new age, will lead toward a diffuse, distracted awareness.

Cathy Davidson of Duke University, in her 2011 book *Now You See It: How the Brain Science of Attention Will Transform the Way We Live, Work, and Learn*, argues that the new distracted awareness being engendered in young people these days, the Millennial generation who are digital natives, is in fact a new awakening, a new twenty-first-century way of paying attention that is more suited to our current digital age. Yet there are others, such as learning expert Annie Murphy Paul (who has written extensively about how people learn) and the late Stanford University professor and renowned authority on human-computer interaction Clifford Nass, who make the argument that those who support this new type of attention in the cyber world tend to ignore the inflexible and near-universal limits of our working memory that allow us to hold only a few items of information in our awareness at any one time, while also ignoring the fact that human cognition is ill suited for attending to multiple streams of information and for simultaneously performing multiple tasks.

Needless to say, this particular debate is going to take place for any number of years as cognition experts, neuroscientists, and experts in learning study the effects of the cyber age on our minds and brains, as well as learning more about how people are specifically adapting to the Internet and to all of their digital devices.

However, relative to the subject of this book, which is the potentially deleterious effects that our new Internet age might have upon the subtle creativity of mind necessary for pursuing a larger intelligence, one might certainly imagine how a distracted awareness could easily be seen in terms of something even more straightforward and clear: the enemy of the focused intensity necessary for apprehending the nature of one's thinking mind and one's self in order to potentially live beyond them, even if only temporarily. To put the matter in a somewhat trite manner of speaking, one will never be able to multitask his or her way into the world of the limitless.

Yet to understand exactly why this might be true, we need to begin to look more closely at how the digital world and its devices might be affecting not only our thinking minds but also our capacity to clearly understand the process of thought itself, how it works and what its particular limitations are. Clearly relevant to this issue is what our current cyber age might be doing to our working memories and their capacity to attain a better understanding of the tenuous nature of the past.

Our working memories, by their very nature, are something organic. This means that in attempting to recall something that we have temporarily forgotten we necessarily need to follow certain pathways in the neuronal structure of our brains until we can bring the missing piece of information or knowledge to conscious attention. In a very real sense, we are retracing the creation of the memory within our cognitive map until we can clearly retrieve it. One might even say that if we are acutely aware of what is occurring, we are becoming acquainted with the nature of our thinking mind and with the process of thought itself.

In the past, before the advent of the Internet, we would often try to recall information or knowledge by opening a book, magazine, or newspaper that contains facts concerning what we were trying to remember, and then attempt to make the necessary connections. Or we could even call a friend on the phone or ask the people with whom we are living to help us. Or we might try to stop thinking about what we are trying to recall in hopes of clearing the neuronal pathways in our brain that lead toward it. Surely everyone has had the experience of having a forgotten bit of information come clearly to mind minutes after one has stopped trying to recall it.

In all these instances, we are, in a very real sense (if we are attuned to it), getting a lesson about how the processes of thought and memory actually work. Yet when we simply employ some powerful search engine such as Google to immediately bring up the forgotten information, and in so doing outsource our working memory to it, this opportunity (invited or not) to apprehend how thought and memory work as we become directly acquainted with them goes right out the window.

Then, over time, as we become increasingly dependent upon the search engines in our phones or computers to retrieve information for us, not only do we lose this chance to be more directly connected with the dynamics of thought and memory, but there is also a very real chance that some of the pathways in our brain that lead toward specific facts, information, and knowledge will begin to disappear completely simply because they are no longer being traversed. Consequently, the dynamics of our thinking minds and our memories become increasingly inaccessible to us.

For the average person who simply wants to go about his daily life using Google to provide him with facts and information that he can't recall, and who has little or no interest in pursuing an expanded consciousness, content to leave it to people whom he considers mystical or religious in some sense, although his working memory is being negatively affected, this development might seem to him to be far from catastrophic.

Yet for the person who is genuinely interested in learning about the nature of his thinking mind and memory in pursuit of something larger, this development concerning his working memory becomes nothing short of a genuine impediment to this search. He would in a very real sense become like the scientist investigating some aspect of the universe or biological world who has forever lost access to important data.

Gazzaley and Rosen, once again in *The Distracted Mind*, write of how our working memories are characterized by two distinct characteristics: *ca-*

pacity and *fidelity*. Capacity refers to the amount of information being stored, and fidelity to the quality of that stored information—how faithful internal representations of it are to what it actually represents.

In terms of fidelity, it has been demonstrated that there is a rapid rate of decay in the accuracy of information that is stored in both short- and long-term memories; this phenomenon is demonstrated by experiments that have shown how much of a loss of precision of detail occurs between when we become immediately familiar with the information through perception and when it has to be recalled through working memory. Certainly, we have all had the experience of having the vividness of our memory begin to dissipate as we attempt to recall an experience we have recently undergone.

Of course, there is an ongoing debate between neuroscientists, cognitive theorists, psychologists, and others as to how much of this sort of decay in our working memory is simply the result of the passage of time, and how much is caused by some form of interference from our immediate environment. Quite possibly it is the result of both. Either time passes and we tend to forget our experiences in detail or else other experiences come between us and the acuity of what we are trying to recall.

However, as an increasing number of experiments are being conducted, it is also becoming clear to those who study the matter that distraction itself can likewise be a powerful impediment standing between our experiences and our working memories. In one experiment, similar to one Adam Gazzaley conducted in his own lab, subjects were instructed to hold the image of a face in their minds for seven seconds, after which their memory of that face was tested. For some of the subjects, a picture of a different face was flashed on the screen while they were holding the original face in mind. Yet even though these subjects were told prior to the experiment that this would occur, and that this other face was irrelevant and thus should be ignored, their memory of the original face was subtly but consistently reduced, the experiment appearing to demonstrate that the overprocessing of irrelevant information can have a genuine effect on working memory.

So if a mind has learned to be distracted by the flood of information that it takes in every day in the digital world, and if that distracted mind is becoming what those such as Cathy Davidson see it as—a new, distracted awareness that is necessary for coming to grips with the nature of our cyber world—then it seems entirely possible that this new form of distraction might easily become an impediment standing between our experiences and the clarity of our memories in relation to them.

There is also the matter of intelligence itself. Certainly, the depth of our intelligence is dependent upon our ability to access information and knowledge from our working memories so that we can then turn that information and knowledge into actual concepts. Yet, once again, if our working memories are flooded with too much information, it becomes impossible for those memories to be effectively turned into long-term ones that then become part of our reflective consciousness, in which we attempt to think logically about and make sense of our world by forming realistic concepts.

Conceptual thought is in a very real sense how we make sense of our world in relation to ourselves. From studying the Swiss psychologist Jean Piaget, we know that even from a very young age children form concepts about their world that allow them to use their environment in effectively relating to it. For example, at some time between the ages of seven and eleven, children conceptualize the principle of conservation, one in which they come to understand why a certain amount of water that is poured from one container to another is the same amount that it started as.

Yet in order for concepts to become clearly formed within our thinking minds, we also need to have unfettered, clear access to our past experiences. Otherwise, the raw data of experience that underlies those concepts, and without which they couldn't be properly formed, are not as accessible to us as they need to be.

It also means that without clear access to our long-term memories, formed from short-term ones, we're not as able to employ concepts that were formed relative to previous situations in order to understand new situations. In addition, it also means that we're less able to follow the thread of our thoughts, those embedded in our long-term memories, to understand exactly how we came to the concepts that we have developed.

It might also have to do with the capacity to realize that although concepts can certainly give one an accurate picture of reality, they can never be that reality itself simply because our sensory experiences will always occur prior to our capacity to mentally grasp them. That is, there will always be a certain lag between the two.

In order to fully realize the fundamental difference between thought and reality, one must necessarily be able to follow the process of one's thoughts by actually stepping outside of them, even if only temporarily, in order to realize that genuine freedom from one's conditioning can come about only when one is free from the boundaries imposed by his or her thinking mind. And because thought can never become acquainted with what is unknown simply because it is forever a product of one's past experiences, it can never experience the possibility of a larger, more expansive consciousness that might exist beyond the boundaries of rational thought.

These are obviously heady ideas, but not ones that are necessarily impossible to gasp. That is, as long as the process of distraction does not inevitably stand between our experiences and our thoughts and memories. Yet the distracted mind that is now being conditioned into people not only by how they use their digital devices but also by the algorithms that are built into powerful search engines that control and direct people's attention may have now become, whether we realize it or not, a direct adversary of our potential search for an expansive, more insightful awareness. Yet to put this into a clearer context, it might be necessary to examine exactly what relationship our conditioned digital minds might have to the process of thought itself.

The digital memories in our computers, tablets, or phones are based on our past responses to information or knowledge. Whether we are searching for something on Google, trolling Twitter or Facebook for potential connections, shopping on Amazon, or simply looking for music in iTunes, the memories inside our devices, as we all know, are able to immediately recognize who we are in terms of our past relationship to information. This means, of course, that we are constantly drawn back to our past.

This might also mean that as our minds become increasingly conditioned by the Internet, we are becoming ever more bound to the process of thought itself, which, as was mentioned earlier, moves like a pendulum swinging incessantly between past, present, and future, yet one that always originates in the past. Then, of course, as we become ever more a product of our past, we become less able to realize how thoroughly conditioned we all are simply because, for that to occur, direct insight into those quiet spaces that exist beyond the boundaries of the thinking mind is required.

The real danger, of course, is that the same sort of conditioned, limited mind-set might be occurring whether we are online, texting on our smartphone, or simply taking a walk around the neighborhood. That is, the conditioning that has already been inculcated within us by the digital world remains with us regardless of how much we use the Internet. In other words, the damage to our psyches has already been done.

For example, our distracted minds, which now move at such a speed while we are online, are habitually less able to be still and, in so doing, are less able to ascertain what truths may exist within that stillness. Or, as we become increasingly conditioned to access some search engine in order to acquire information or knowledge, the pathways we might have previously employed to fish the information out of our working memories become ever more inaccessible; as that process occurs, our understanding of how the processes of thought and memory occur become ever more of a mystery.

Of course, there is also the very real danger that as the digital world increasingly becomes the very center of commerce, business transactions, personal or social relations, the arts, politics, or most everything else, all of us by necessity will have to live in that world whether we want to or not. As a result, there will be no way to avoid having our minds and brains conditioned by it simply because we have now become part of it. Consequently, our thinking minds may well begin to lose the capacity to reflect on the nature of thought itself while seeking the still mind that leads toward an expansive awareness.

Although there is still not a great deal written or researched about how the Internet is changing our brains at the physiological level to the point that our intelligence and our reflective consciousness might be negatively affected, at the same time quite a bit of indirect evidence would appear to exist for how this might occur.

While studying the brain of the sea slug, Nobel Prize–winning scientist Eric Kandel found that the number of synapses in the brain is not fixed. It changes with learning, something that Kandel found was true not just of sea slugs but also for other animals, including primates. In looking at the molecular changes that occur in the brain's synapses as short-term memories are formed, he and his researchers found that certain types of cells called interneurons are instrumental in this process; the interneurons produce serotonin, which fine-tunes the synaptic connections. Then, through a complex chemical process, the resulting synaptic changes are concentrated at certain regions on the surface of one of the brain's neurons and perpetuated over long periods of time. As a result of the chemical and genetic signals and changes that occur in the synapses, they become able to hold memories over the course of days, even years. As Kandel says, "The growth and maintenance of new synaptic terminals makes memory persist."

Furthermore, as neuroscientists have known for some time now, the plasticity of our brains continually shapes both our behavior and our identity. Yet that plasticity of the brain, its capacity to physiologically change through learning and experience, may have provided us with something just as important—something that may be the key to understanding thought, memory, and the past. This is the dynamic of how transitory and illusive changes in our physical brains brought on by thought and memory can in fact be.

Susan Greenfield writes in *Mind Change* of how mere thinking can actually change the physical brain. Citing a study conducted by Alvaro Pascual-Leone and his research group in 1995, Greenfield writes of how, over a five-day period during which a control group learned to play the piano using five-finger exercises, there was an astonishing change in their brain scans. Yet what was even more remarkable was that another group of people who were part of the same experiment, and who were required to only imagine that they were playing the piano, showed almost identical changes in their brain scans as those who were actually playing with the finger exercises.

Another example of these surprising effects of mere thinking on the physical brain that Greenfield points to is the well-known placebo effect, in which simply the belief that an inert substance has therapeutic properties can be enough to cure an illness due to naturally occurring morphine chemicals that are set off by positive thoughts. Cognitive behavioral therapy for patients suffering from depression has been found to work in much the same manner. That is, as the therapist is able to get the patient to visualize a different context for his maladies and problems, this process can trigger certain chemical reactions in the brain that aid in lifting the depression.

If mere thoughts or pictures in one's mind can actually trigger significant physiological changes in the brain, then it would appear to be important that we question the reality of memories embedded in our brains in relation to the thinking mind and ask whether our memories of the past, as those such as Marcel Proust claim to have discovered, are only as real as our constant capacity to change them with our thoughts.

In addition, if we are to begin to examine the potentially fallible nature of memory, then surely our long-term memories need to be as accessible to us as possible so that we might examine their illusive nature. This is in fact the great irony of examining the nature of thought and memory in pursuit of a larger intelligence—that in order to possibly transcend the boundaries of thought, memory, and the past in seeking that larger consciousness, those things must first be available to us in their clearest incantations.

If the digital world is causing long-term memories to become increasingly inaccessible simply because our short-term memories are being flooded with too much information on the Internet, then this would appear to be an obvious impediment to that search for a larger awareness that exists beyond the boundaries of the self, memory, and our thinking minds.

There is also the issue of creative thinking, the capacity to make significant connections between different pieces of knowledge or information where before none existed. It also means developing the capacity to focus intently on potential creative connections that one may have drawn before pursuing them wherever they may lead.

If a distracted awareness facilitated today by the Internet and digital devices is in fact affecting people's capacity for creative thought, and likewise their capacity to fully attend to those creative thoughts in pursuit of them, then there may in fact be a huge irony at the center of this new digital age that we have now entered.

As the cyber world allows us to more fully connect with others, and to pursue creative ideas during this communication, at the same time our capacity for deeply creative thinking may be in the process of being diluted by the way we are using our digital devices, and by a World Wide Web that offers so many opportunities for creativity in the external world even as it may be dulling the capacity for creativity within us. So this is what we will focus on next: creative thinking in relation to a potential digital barrier that might impede such creativity.

Chapter Six

Creative Thought and the Digital Barrier

The late Clifford Nass, former professor of communication at Stanford University who was part of an extensive research study on multitasking, studied the effects that multitasking might have on people's ability to concentrate, particularly on their capacity to focus on just one thing when they are required to do so, his studies demonstrating the negative effect that chronic multitasking has on one's capacity for this type of focused attention. In addition, Nass's research convinced him that such divided attention spans also affect creativity because of the hard work and focus it takes to bring a creative thought to fruition.

In the same vein, Annie Murphy Paul, in an article that appeared in a 2013 issue of the *Hechinger Report*, "The New Marshmallow Test: Resisting the Temptations of the Web," after she studied the research of psychologists and others concerning how young people are using their digital devices while learning, writes of how students who can't resist multitasking on their devices while doing their schoolwork not only tend to understand and remember less but also, and even more important relative to the capacity to think creatively, *have greater difficulty transferring their learning to newer contexts*. This development means a diminished capacity to creatively transfer what they might have learned in one area of study to another.

Well-known Hungarian psychologist Mihaly Csikszentmihalyi has written of how creative thinkers tend to be those who exist in a state of flow in which they are absorbed in whatever task they are engaged because their particular skill level and the level of the task in which they are absorbed not

only are perfectly matched but also exist at a high level—a state of concentration or complete absorption with the particular task at hand that some
people have referred to as "being in the zone."

In his book *Creativity: Flow and the Psychology of Discovery and Invention*, Csikszentmihalyi writes of how in order to awaken creative energy we
must erect barriers against distraction, dig channels so that energy can flow
more freely, and find ways to escape interruptions. If we do not, he goes on
to say, entropy is sure to break down the concentration that the pursuit of an
interest requires, thought then returning to the vague, unfocused, constantly
distracted condition that it may have been in previously.

What the ideas of all three of these investigators of learning, attention,
and memory have in common is the notion that for creative thought to exist it
must take place within a psychological space akin to Csikszentmihalyi's flow
state in which the mind is able to make consistent connections between
different areas of knowledge and information without any sort of interruptions or distraction preventing those connections from being apprehended.
Otherwise, the absorption necessary for creatively connecting different facts
or ideas will be inherently missing.

Needless to say, this model for creativity is something that is necessarily
at variance with the high-powered interruption machines that are the Internet
and our digital devices—those that dole out information and knowledge to us
not in a steady stream, but rather in the form of isolated pieces of information
that often break our concentration into bits of unrelated knowledge. In the
process, our minds are becoming ever more conditioned and less able to sink
fully into whatever new information or knowledge we encounter in the form
of the written word.

Add to that how search engines such as Google are using powerful algorithms to direct our attention as we surf the Web to the advertising that will
bring them increasing sources of revenue, and you truly have a technology
and artificial reality that is directly at variance with the flow state necessary
for making the sort of connections that might allow us not only to think
creatively but also to comprehend the potential relationship between creativity itself and our thinking minds or to allow ourselves to surrender to Alan
Watts's *stream of life* in search of a limitless world that might exist on the
other side of thought.

In point of fact, due to the interruption machine that is the Internet,
Csikszentmihalyi's flow state would seem to now be in danger of being
conditioned out of our psyches, which means that consciousness itself (which

Watts refers to as a stream of experiences, sensations, thoughts, and feelings in constant motion) is in danger of being seriously interrupted by the distracted awareness being inculcated in us by the Internet, where bits of information and knowledge arrive in a thoroughly fragmented manner.

As a result of this, the conflict within us between our desire for permanence in our lives, that which arises from our insecurity and our need to hold onto those things that we deem solid and imperishable, and the reality that life itself is by its very nature always in a state of ever-changing flux will be inevitably heightened, causing us out of our own insecurity to resist both the stream of life and the river of thought all the more. Consequently, our potential journey toward a more expansive state of mind in accordance with the never-ending flux of life may easily become blocked.

Once again, as Alan Watts writes in *The Wisdom of Insecurity*, we are conditioned to confuse the intelligible with the fixed. That is, we think that making sense of the details of our lives is impossible unless the flow of events can somehow be fitted into a framework of fixed ideas, thoughts, and scientific laws that we can control and that these things are representative of some unchanging reality that exists on the other side of the flux of our daily lives.

It's as if we are forever attempting to dam a powerful river whose flow can never be impeded. Consequently, we're forever unable to glimpse what may be the larger reality to which that metaphorical river might lead us.

By breaking information and knowledge into ever smaller bits as it creates a distracted awareness within us, the Internet is the ultimate tool available to us for the purpose of controlling the eternal flux through the fragmented mental activities that it engenders in us. As we jump between webpages, text messages, or fragments of different stories that more and more people are now often only scanning these days rather than reading thoroughly, we are indeed conditioning our minds to move further and further away from Csikszentmihalyi's flow state and from Alan Watts's stream of life.

There is also something else: the disappearance in our digital age of the quiet spaces within people's minds necessary for both creative thought and direct insight. Recent imaging studies of people have found that major sections of their brains become surprisingly active during quiet periods when they aren't involved in their daily activities, these studies suggesting to researchers that periods of rest are critical in allowing the brain to make creative connections between different ideas that have been recently assimilated.

Yet, obviously, as more and more people today spend an increasing amount of time on their digital devices, they tend to spend significantly less quiet time in the space of their mind relative to the time they spend online staring into the plastic screen of their iPhones or computers, relentlessly searching for fragmented bits of information. As a result, they are not allowing their brain the quiet time it needs to think creatively.

In an article that appeared in *A Journal for the Association for Psychological Science*, one that was based on prior research of theirs, John Kounios, professor of psychology at Drexel University, and Mark Jung-Beeman, of Northwestern University, revealed a greater capacity in a group of subjects to creatively solve a series of anagrams when their right brain activity, that associated with creative insight, was at a higher level during a resting state they had experienced just before attempting the anagrams. This finding obviously suggests that the capacity for creativity inherent in individuals may occur even while they are daydreaming or while their minds are at rest.

Therefore, if people do indeed need to rest their minds in this manner in order to make the sort of creative connections that are not only necessary for apprehending a certain area more completely but also vital to achieving the sort of expanded consciousness alluded to in this particular work, and their awareness is being continually distracted by the Internet and digital devices in the manner in which certain neuroscientists and cognitive theorists say that it is, then this situation almost certainly is going to have a profound effect on the ability of people to think creatively. It will also affect their potential capacity to creatively expand their conscious mind toward a larger intelligence.

Likewise, seemingly relevant to how the current Internet age may be affecting people's creative capacities is the issue of how the digital world is causing their visual skills relative to taking in information and knowledge to increase, while their critical thinking and analysis skills have simultaneously declined. According to research undertaken by Patricia Greenfield, distinguished professor of psychology at UCLA, learning itself has changed due to technology.

Her studies confirm that by using more visual media, students in our current age will process information better. However, she goes on to say, most visual media, like what one increasingly finds on the Internet (such as YouTube or in online video games), do not allow for reflection, analysis, or imagination as does the quiet reading or simple listening that develops imagination, induction, reflection, and critical thinking.

Among the studies Greenfield undertook was a classroom study showing that students who were given access to the Internet during class and were encouraged to use it during lectures, rather than simply listen to the speaker, did not process what the speaker said as well as those students who did not have Internet access.

In another study of Greenfield's, she found that those students who watched "CNN Headline News" with just the news anchor on the screen, without the "news crawl" at the bottom, remembered significantly more facts than those who watched with the distraction of the crawling text augmented by additional stock market and weather information.

There is also the issue of how increasingly information is being turned into visual art in the form of *data art*. By taking data, even that to be found within the highly mathematical world of algorithms, and turning it into "art" that can be apprehended visually, data artists are attempting to give people a more direct, visual connection with information that data in its literal form doesn't provide, the true objective of data art being to create aesthetic forms and artistic works that reflect the data they represent.

From a poster similar to a Jackson Pollack splatter painting designed to raise awareness about the Amazon rainforest by visually representing its destruction, to a futuristic looking engineered natural garden that depicts people's movements on the Web, the idea is to present information and data to people entirely through their visual sense, even though the data itself originates in the world of graphics, simulations, worksheets, and statistics. In other words, those who get their "information" from data art can bypass the world of the written word completely while apprehending it directly with their senses.

Yet as enticing as visual presentations on the Web such as those that appear on YouTube, Instagram, or data art are, the point that seemingly needs to be considered is that if people today are increasingly getting their information and knowledge in short bursts within the visual realm, rather than by quietly reading long passages or listening intently to a speaker, then it seems entirely possible that the quiet spaces in our minds vital to creative thought and analysis are being continually eroded.

In point of fact, as people increasingly watch a video online that gives them encapsulated versions of the facts in which they are interested, rather than apprehending the same information by focusing intently on an extended passage of writing, those quiet internal spaces may be increasingly in danger of disappearing.

At the same time, fluency with written language and the capacity to think creatively, to be able to make significant connections within a broad field of knowledge, are vitally related. Without the first, the second can't possibly flourish, something that is evident in the simultaneous development of the written word and scientific/artistic thought and its creations throughout history. As the written word became increasingly complex, so did people's capacity for creative thinking.

The great media critic Marshall McLuhan postulated the idea that before the advent of the written word, when communication between people was entirely oral in nature, people enjoyed what he believed was a relationship with words based entirely on their sensorial or emotive experience. However, as people learned to read, they became more detached from this emotive, sensory side of themselves.

Yet at the same time, he believed that the written word freed people from the need to use only their memories to define their experiences simply because a definition of their experience could now be written down. Consequently, the written word opened their minds to much broader frontiers of thought and creative expression.

Eventually, this increased capacity for creative thought that is linked to the written word came to fruition in the nineteenth and twentieth centuries with two towering works of intellectual achievement—Charles Darwin's *Origin of the Species* and Albert Einstein's theory of general relativity. Specifically, the subtlety and power of Darwin's brilliant idea of natural selection related to the evolution of different species and Einstein's incredible idea that a fabric of space-time is the driving force in the universe are both extreme, vivid examples of how explorations of the frontiers of the creative world are necessarily dependent upon the clarity that the written word provides to unleash them.

Even more so, the states of mind and being to which brilliant metaphysical thinkers such as Krishnamurti, Lao Tzu, Alan Watts, or David Bohm point to necessarily rely on the clarity of the written word to unleash them exactly because such states of existence are necessarily beyond the bounds of thought and language themselves.

Krishnamurti continually explored the idea that the thinker and the thought are inherently one and the same and that the separation of these two is what creates conflict in us, as well as subservience to the boundaries of the self. Alan Watts wrote of how any separate "I" that thinks thoughts and experiences experience is an illusion. And David Bohm wrote of how it is the boundary of language itself that prevents us from perceiving what he refers to as the implicate order in everything. Obviously, in order to begin to understand what these men were referring to one must first be able to touch the function of thought and language at their innermost, most revealing levels.

Yet if we are moving toward a world where people receive information and knowledge increasingly from digital sites that are exclusively visual, where might this trend potentially lead? Will we be entering a world where communication, facts, and ideas become largely visual in nature? And in the process, will people's capacity for not only creative thinking but also a potential exploration of the frontiers of consciousness become increasingly limited by the replacement of written expression with visual images?

As those who study how people learn, such as Tesia Marshik (professor of psychology at the University of Wisconsin–La Crosse) or Annie Murphy Paul, discover that the idea of people possessing different learning styles is in fact a myth, the idea that so-called visual learners will be able to absorb information and knowledge better on exclusively visual sites like YouTube is being debunked. Instead, what scientists and writers like Marshik and Paul are discovering is that most of what we learn is stored in terms of meaning, not through visual images. That is, in order for an image to be retained as information or knowledge, it must first be meaningful to the person who is apprehending it.

Yet one must wonder that if more and more people are going directly to sites like YouTube or any number of other primarily visual sites prevalent on social media, rather than apprehending the relevant images only after they have first uncovered their meaning through knowledge associated with the written word, how will that affect their capacity to find the meanings behind the information they are encountering?

Eventually, could we end up living in a world where the vast majority of people are merely content to absorb facts and bits of information without bothering to think critically about the meaning and significance on which these might rest simply because they are apprehending their knowledge and information primarily visually? One can only imagine the collective shallow consciousness that might result if this ever became the case—a collective mindset that is the very antithesis of the search for a limitless intelligence that only a few people, up to this point in time, have been brave enough to undertake.

The meaning behind information, data, and knowledge will always be what is significant about these things, not their mere external representations.

Yet without the mind-set to dive deeply into the meaning of things, those meanings will be rarely, if ever, uncovered. The late, noted psychotherapist Victor Frankl wrote in his iconic book *Man's Search for Meaning* that our primary drive in life is not pleasure, as Sigmund Freud maintained, but the pursuit of what we personally find meaningful.

A Holocaust survivor and a prisoner at Auschwitz at the end of World War II, Frankl developed his approach to psychological healing known as *logotherapy* largely from his concentration camp experiences. After enduring the suffering to which he was subjected in the camp, he claimed to have realized that even in the midst of the most absurd, painful, and dehumanizing situations, life has meaning. In addition, and most important, Frankl concluded that a lack of meaning in people's lives is the paramount cause of existential stress. In fact, he believed that modern-day neurosis, as much as anything, is essentially a crisis of meaninglessness originating from an existential vacuum characterized by boredom, apathy, and emptiness and that people without meaning in their lives can easily be exposed to depression and addiction.

Whether or not one agrees with Frankl that the pursuit of meaning is life's primary drive, and that contemporary neurosis is essentially a function of lack of meaning, it seems important to consider whether the manner in which people might be increasingly coming into contact with the superficial exterior of information and knowledge when they go online and apprehend it only visually, rather than diving fully into the knowledge by reading it at a greater depth, might be having an actual effect on their capacity to find meaning in their lives.

In other words, in a cyber world in which people can communicate with others more easily than they did before, and with much greater speed, is the price for this ease and rapidity of communication a superficiality that might be engendered in many of us by a digital age that is shallower and more superficial than previous ages even as it is broader and more expansive?

That is, in order to find meaning in our lives is it necessary to maintain our capacity to dive deeply into thoughts and words? And is the Internet significantly and negatively affecting that ability? If both of these things are true, then it seems entirely possible that our digital age might at one and the same time be causing people to become both more superficial and more neurotic in the manner to which Victor Frankl alluded due to a less meaningful existence.

By the end of the sixteenth century, due to the invention of the printing press and moveable type, complex scientific information that was part of the fields of astronomy, anatomy, and physics was suddenly available to anyone who could read. Consequently, the world was suddenly filled with new fascinating information and previously unreachable abstract experience. According to Neil Postman, this development required new skills, new attitudes, and especially a new type of consciousness, one that involved an enriched capacity for conceptual thought, intellectual vigor, and a passion for clarity.

In other words, there was suddenly a need for clarity of thought that had been previously unnecessary when most people received their information secondhand through rulers and religious leaders simply because people were now more able to read and think for themselves. Ultimately, this new need for clarity reached the point that even those who speculated on the meaning of the universe and life itself were able to do so through the power of rational thought as all sorts of superstitions and vague falsehoods that had been the creation of the church were eventually left far behind.

In fact, it was man's capacity to read and then take his thoughts to a point of completion that produced the clarity that led to a new radical apprehension of the physical universe conceived by Einstein with his relativity theory, and by Niels Bohr and Werner Heisenberg with their uncovering of quantum reality, and to the understanding of the startling relationship that might exist between universal truth and the mind itself that was probed by those such as Krishnamurti or Alan Watts with their metaphysical speculations.

Certainly, one has to be extremely precise in one's thinking in order to comprehend how time and space might in fact be one and the same; to understand how the participation of the observer actually changes his observations in the quantum world of the extremely small to the point that he can no longer perceive the reality with which he is endeavoring to be in touch; or to understand how within our own minds the observer is in fact the observed, or the thinker the thought. That is, it is the depth of thought and the clarity of words that allow one to enter worlds that necessarily exist beyond thoughts and words.

Yet through the influence of the Internet, where information and knowledge is increasingly transmitted to our visual sense, our passion for the meaning of words and thoughts might become diluted. This then, it would seem, might become a significant loss relative to our potential search for the sort of expansive consciousness that requires a mind that is quiet because it has ultimately transcended thoughts and words in the search for meaning by first becoming intensely familiar with what they have to teach us.

Chapter Seven

Art and Culture in the Digital Age

The late, great writer Susan Sontag used to say, "Love words/agonize over sentences/pay attention to the world." Although her statement may indeed be open to different interpretations, what she most likely meant by her prescient admonition was that the depth at which one reads and writes can easily determine the degree to which one is able to immerse oneself in the details of the world in which one lives. And certainly it is possible to read her essays, with her complex, brilliant sentences that draw one ever more acutely into the subject matter about which she is writing—be it the message engendered by the photographic image, the metaphors associated with illness, or the dangers of interpreting art—and come away thinking about and experiencing the particulars of one's life with an increased level of scrutiny.

Similarly, one is able to grasp the richness of existing in the world by reading the great stream-of-consciousness writers like Marcel Proust, Virginia Woolf, Jack Kerouac, or Henry Miller, or writers like Leo Tolstoy or Gustav Flaubert, with their complicated story lines and deep levels of characterization. In addition, one has ample opportunity to dive into not just the bottom-line, existential realities of life in the world but also the psychology of one's self by reading masters of literature like Dostoevsky or Shakespeare.

Yet a 2013 article in the *New York Times* by Tamar Lewin describes how college students are currently fleeing from humanities studies like rats off a sinking ship. One of the reasons given for this development, a more obvious one, is that students are preferring to take STEM-related courses that they feel will better prepare them for permanent employment in a world that is increasingly technologically driven, rather than waste time, as many of them see it, taking courses in literature or philosophy that offer them only a marginal level of job security. In fact, it has been reported lately that not only is enrollment in STEM courses far exceeding enrollment in humanities classes, but young people are now actually reading books related to science far more than they are reading literature or philosophy.

Naturally, in our current technologically advanced job market, one that exists in a period of high unemployment, it is entirely understandable why young people are choosing to study science and technology as opposed to reading literature or philosophy. Yet at the same time, it seems possible that job opportunities may not be the sole reason why students now have their noses in books having to do with science and technology, as opposed to reading Dostoevsky, Camus, or Shakespeare.

This trend may likewise have very much to do with the effects of the Internet and certain digital devices on the minds of young people who have grown up as digital natives in our current information age. That is, the distracted awareness that is being engendered in many of them.

Quite simply, it may have to do with the fact that reading *Crime and Punishment*, *The Plague*, or *Hamlet* requires the capacity for deep reading and deep thinking over a sustained period of time. That is, one simply cannot fully apprehend either the power or the intelligence of these great works unless one is able to dive completely into them. There isn't any way that one will be able to genuinely absorb, enjoy, or appreciate these works if one is not able to stay with the long arc of their stories, their highly complex character development, or their extreme moral and ethical complexities over an extended period.

Of course, the same distracted awareness that has been alluded to earlier in this work, one that affects people's ability to focus on complex material, or even on material that is more basic, is an awareness that is being engendered not just in college students but in all of us lately by the Web and digital technologies, potentially causing many of us to have less interest than people previously did in staying with challenging works of literature until one has completely absorbed them.

There is also the issue of whether a visual image apprehended on a plastic screen stimulates one's impressions to the same extent as its counterpart in the real world does. That is, a number of people, particularly young people who are digital natives, might be accepting a shallower apprehension of their world due to the effects on their minds and brains wrought by their digital devices as they likewise begin to accept a more diluted form of their emotive, impressionistic lives.

And if this is so, would it then mean that future generations might not be able to experience Debussy's deeply impressionistic *Prelude to the After-noon of a Faun*, Bob Dylan's great apocalyptic rock poem *Highway 61 Revisited*, or one of those incredible snow scenes painted by Monet with the same degree of intensity?

What seemingly needs to be studied, relative to this question, is whether there is a significant difference between the emotive depth that a virtual image on a computer screen or on the plastic screen of a phone leaves in someone and the depth which that image's counterpart in the real world leaves. Does the second take place inside someone with significantly greater intensity? If such is indeed the case, then this new cyber world full of digital images might have a profound effect on how fully people apprehend and appreciate the visual or auditory arts such as painting, music, or film.

In addition, if digital images in fact do not leave the same strong impression in us as their corresponding counterparts in the real world, and if we are spending more and more time in the digital world, are our emotive lives growing increasingly dulled and diluted?

As we increasingly apprehend a plethora of digital images on our phones and computers, as compared to experiencing different aspects of the real world purely and directly, isn't there a danger that we will accept the diluted strength of those virtual images as the norm, and thus begin to unconsciously draw a line inside ourselves for how strongly our experiences in the real world might affect us? And if this is potentially so, what effect might this have on our capacity to fully experience great, powerful art?

In order to appreciate a work of art or literature to the fullest, two dynamics would appear to be significant in the mind and emotions of the person who is apprehending the particular work: mental focus and impressionistic depth, the first having mainly to do with great literature, while the second has more to do with music and the visual arts.

So it would seem what needs to be investigated in terms of the potentially deleterious effects that the digital world might have upon the arts and culture is whether our current cyber world and its devices are distracting people's attention while also diluting the depth of their impressions in relation to significant art works.

Lately, two professors at Vassar University have been investigating the effect that people's use of digital devices might be having on their apprehension of literature. Ron Patkus, an adjunct associate professor of history and head of special collections at the Vassar Library, and Susan Zlotnick, an English professor and dean of freshman, have been comparing notes on what they have felt has been less-than-ideal student engagement in Patkus's "Bible as Book" course, and Zlotnick's "Nineteenth-Century British Novel" course.

Together, the two began to wonder whether, because they both teach complex historical materials that require long stretches of concentration, the unresponsiveness of students to readings they were assigned might be due to some shift in their reading skills brought on by their digital habits. In particular, they wondered whether the many continual disruptions engendered by the digital world, from text messaging to a compulsive need to check social media sites, might in fact be affecting the depth into which students were able to dive while reading the literature they were being asked to read, with the significant question being: Have the students really experienced the literature they read in the way it's meant to be experienced?

In conjunction with this question, of course, is the expectation of immediacy that our hyper-digital culture is fostering not just in college students and Millennials but in all of us, stimulating people to excessively multitask. Tom Olsen, associate professor of English at SUNY New Paltz, who teaches Shakespeare and other complex works of literature to his students, attributes the shortening of attention spans he has seen in his students' absorption of what they are reading to what he terms a "fear of missing out," something many young people now refer to as FOMO. That is, students sitting near their phone wondering what might be coming their way on email, text messaging, or social media while they're attempting to immerse themselves in *Hamlet* or *King Lear* may have caused their concentrated reading to suffer.

Obviously, this effect tends to be more acute for those in their twenties due to their richer social lives, but the same dynamic of not being able to concentrate on a work of literature due to what might be suddenly appearing on one's smartphone is becoming increasingly true for all of us.

If a distracted awareness is being engendered in people not only because they might be anticipating the arrival of a new text message or email on their phone but also because the Internet is causing them to approach information and knowledge in a shallower, more fragmented manner (that which has been alluded to earlier in this particular work), then how is this going to affect their acquaintance with great literature? In short, are our physiological brains being hardwired by the way we use the Internet and our digital devices in a manner that over time will make it more difficult for us to sink into a work by Shakespeare or Dostoevsky?

In point of fact, what are the specific characteristics of a work of great literature that make it powerful and profound, and how might the potential negative effects that our addictive use of the Internet may be having on our minds and physiological brains be somehow either diluting these characteristics or preventing people from fully accessing them?

Rick Gekoski, a freelance writer who writes about books and book buying, in a 2011 article that appeared in *The Guardian* identified what he considered some of the characteristics that make a work of literature great. Among these were high quality of the language, complexity of theme and detail, universality, depth, quality of feeling, memorableness, and readability. He adds that when you read a work of literature that possesses these particular qualities, you feel that your internal planes have somehow shifted and that things will never be quite the same again.

Certainly, Dostoevsky's *Crime and Punishment*, one of the greatest works of literature ever written, possesses many (if not all) of these characteristics. For one, its complex thematic structure is nearly unparalleled. It is an intense psychological drama having to do with the mind of a character dealing with his own guilt concerning his "existential" act of murder while attempting to maintain some semblance of sanity. It is also an enthralling murder mystery in which the murderer is not only the hero of the story but also known as the murderer by the reader from the outset, as well as a study of social class in late nineteenth-century Russia, a philosophical novel that endlessly traverses the boundary between good and evil, and even a heartfelt, surprising, offbeat love story involving two downtrodden people.

In short, not only is *Crime and Punishment*'s theme incredibly complex with powerful depth, but it also deals with issues that are universal relative to the human condition. It is likewise incredibly heartfelt relative to the intense inner lives of the characters, which it reveals despite also being a philosophical novel, in addition to being as compulsively readable as a novel can be, dwarfing many of our contemporary "real page-turner" mysteries.

So how might some of the effects on people by their use of digital devices in our current Internet age be possibly impeding their full enjoyment of and contact with some of the characteristics of a great work of literature such as *Crime and Punishment*?

For one, if people are growing more conditioned to skimming along the surface of what they are reading in order to quickly acquire bits of information, as many people do who spend a significant amount of time reading online, rather than sinking into a piece of writing like a scuba diver (to use Nicholas Carr's terminology), then there is no doubt that if they carry that similar mindset to Dostoevsky's great work, they will never be able to sink fully into the inner lives of the great anti-hero Raskolnikov or Sonya, the prostitute with the innocent heart who eventually saves him.

Similarly, if people's capacity to turn short-term recollections into long-term memories grows diminished as their short-term memories suffer from information overload in our current Internet age, their capacity for conceptualization, that which is dependent upon being able to create an internal mapping of one's world in the brain's hippocampus region, will likewise almost certainly suffer. As a result, when they read some great work like *Crime and Punishment*, with its universal truths rolled into one work, many of those truths may become increasingly inaccessible to them due to their diminished capacity to conceptualize.

Finally, a great work like Dostoevsky's, if one is able to sink fully into it, becomes extremely memorable. Yet if many people are now outsourcing their working memories to things like Google or Echo by employing these sites or devices to immediately call up information they can't immediately access, rather than searching the pathways of their brains for such information or knowledge, might something like *Crime and Punishment* grow less memorable to them over time?

Then, lastly, there is of course the issue of how much the distracted awareness that neuroscientists and others are noticing is being engendered in people by how they use their digital devices might affect readers' ability to stay with a lengthy, complex work of great literature like *Crime and Punishment* over a sustained period of time without giving up before the book is completely read and fully apprehended.

Likewise, of course, is the question of what effect our current Internet age and how people are using their digital devices might have on their apprehension of painting, sculpting, film, music, or other arts that have a primarily sensorial foundation.

Once again, might those who spend a significant amount of time staring into a plastic screen where artificial images or pictures do not leave as powerful an impression as their counterparts in the real world be subject to having their emotive lives somehow stifled as they grow increasingly conditioned to possessing diluted sensibilities by their continual apprehension of exclusively virtual images? And then, as a result, might their interaction with great painting, music, sculpting, or film be correspondingly stifled?

In his essay "Emotions, Cyberspace and the 'Virtual' Body: A Critical Appraisal," Simon J. Williams, professor of sociology at the University of Warwick in London, England, discusses the flattening or deadening effect that computer representations have on the imagination. That is, no computer program or package, however real or sophisticated it might seem, is going to offer the range of options for experiencing the many aspects of the real world such as one might encounter through a simple walk in the woods.

What cyberspace does, according to Williams, is limit the imagination by forcing it to walk along certain paths and not others, reducing it to a function of technology by narrowing down the rich plurality of our experiences. This is exactly what can cause a virtual image on a plastic screen to dull our experience in comparison with how we might experience its real-world counterpart—that our potential range of responses to whatever we are apprehending becomes limited by the static image itself. As a result, as more and more people now connect with their world or with others through virtual images, they can easily become conditioned to having their emotive lives diluted by a more limited range of responses to their real-life experiences.

Consequently, when people look at a great painting or sculpture in a museum (or even one hanging on the wall of their home), take in a great film, watch a great work of modern dance, or go to a symphony or jazz concert, over time, because they have become so accustomed to taking in static images on their smartphones rather than presenting themselves with the full range of responses to these same things that might exist in the real world, the range of their internal responses to the art they are witnessing may likewise grow limited, in effect dulling their emotive response to it.

There is also in conjunction with this concern the issue of an embodied self, one that is necessary for one's emotive life to be affected by either great art or life in the real world as much as it might be. That is, if we are not approaching great visual art in a fully embodied manner, it may not leave the same heightened impression upon us that it otherwise might. After all, our emotive reactions to our world and the depth of our impressions when we react to something like a beautiful sunset or the sensitive, delicate nature of another person are in fact highly physical responses to those things, and so it is with being able to fully experience a great work of art.

The nineteenth-century philosopher-psychologist William James had the profound insight that not only does the brain communicate with the body, but the body also communicates with the brain, his idea being that the conscious experience of emotion takes place *after* the body's physiological response to something. Using the example of how when we encounter a potentially dangerous situation, such as meeting a bear in the woods, we experience the emotion of fear only after we have experienced the physiological responses of increased heart rate and respiration, James put forth the radical idea at the time that our emotional reactions have a profoundly embodied basis.

This idea would mean, of course, that our emotional responses to a work of visual art or music in fact might actually begin with our embodied, physical responses to it, and that if one is not experiencing the work in a fully embodied state due to a dulling of his or her sensorial life, then one's emotional reactions to it might become necessarily dulled or diluted.

If it is in fact true that our habitual acquaintance with virtual images on a plastic screen is conditioning many of us to possess a dulled sensibility, and if that same habitual acquaintance is producing a certain amount of disembodied experience when it comes to fully apprehending the visual arts, then our current Internet age might indeed over time have the effect of keeping us at arm's length from certain important works of art. Consequently, people's opportunity to use their impressionistic responses to great works of visual art in order to seek a more expansive awareness may over time become increasingly limited.

There are, of course, any number of great art works that not only serve to heighten people's sensibilities but also provide them with a certain larger awareness concerning life in the world. Vincent Van Gogh's iconic, otherworldly painting *Starry Night* is one, while Beethoven's powerful, dramatic Fifth Symphony or Dvorak's haunting New World Symphony are certainly examples of two other great works pointing toward something larger. So are Dostoevsky's *The Brothers Karamazov* or Friedrich Nietzsche's *Thus Spoke Zarathustra*. And so are any number of Shakespeare's plays, from *King Lear* to *Macbeth*, as well as Peter Weiss's great work of impressionistic, total theater *Marat/Sade*.

What all of these works, and others like them, have in common is that they all point indirectly but powerfully toward a larger, more expansive awareness by affecting one's emotive life to the point that a certain inner state that possesses an intelligence and wholeness on the other side of rational thought begins to manifest itself, meaning that these great works must be experienced primarily impressionistically for them to lead us on this larger, more expansive journey. This, of course, means that one's inner life must be truly alive in order for us to come fully to grips with them and what they might be telling us.

If one is in fact able to take this journey, it is indeed possible for one or more of these great works to take one to a place where his or her experience of the world, the universe, and also one's self becomes heightened to the point that one might begin to peek over the edge, if only temporarily, in apprehending a world that reveals to him a more expansive and profound reality, one that touches the very truths of our human existence.

Yet fully comprehending and appreciating great works of art requires a definite amount of impressionistic insight, the type that allows one to actually experience the powerful, willful triumph over the most intense suffering inherent in Beethoven's Fifth Symphony, which he wrote as he was fully realizing that he was losing the one thing that was most precious to him: his hearing. Or to comprehend the almost exquisite aloneness that one must endure to become free of one's worldly conditioning in search of a genuine independent spirit that is at the heart of Nietzsche's *Zarathustra*. Or the nearly mad craving for the beauty of the physical world that is at the epicenter of so many of Van Gogh's paintings.

Yet making a connection between the strength of impressions that a great work of art might engender and a more expansive awareness toward which that work of art might lead means that one must have the ability to make that connection with genuine insight into where the artist is leading him or her.

So this is where we will journey next—toward a discussion of the nature of insight relative to both artistic expression and that larger consciousness toward which great works of art often inevitably lead, and likewise toward how those particular dynamics might be threatened by our current Internet age.

Chapter Eight

Insight, Art, and a Higher Awareness

Eric Kandel, in addition to providing the world with his probing quest over the years to understand the physiological basis of memory, has likewise studied and written about the psychology of visual perceptions and emotional responses to art in his brilliant, comprehensive study *The Age of Insight: The Quest to Understand the Unconscious in Art, Mind, and Brain*. In this book, building on the work of those such as Freud or those from the Vienna School of Medicine who eventually influenced others in the Vienna School of Art History, Kandel asks how a viewer might respond to a work of art, particularly a painting, not only from the standpoint of psychology but also in terms of brain biology. In short, he is asking what the physiological basis of insight is.

Writing about how those who have studied exactly how moments of creative insight occur, Kandel mentions in his book how those cognitive psychologists who have studied the matter, such as Mark Jung-Beeman at Northwestern University and John Kounios at Drexel University (working in collaboration with each other), have determined that sudden moments of insight occur in the right hemisphere of the brain. In this regard, Kandel likewise references the work of the late Canadian psychologist Donald O. Hebb, who pointed out that for there to be a true moment of sudden, creative insight, the task it involves needs to possess just the right degree of difficulty for the person having the insight.

Obviously, Hebb's ideas on creative insight are closely related to those of Mihaly Csikszentmihalyi and his flow state, that state of intense concentration which occurs when someone is completely absorbed in the activity or situation at hand, and which, according to Csikszentmihalyi, can only occur when the challenge of the task and the skill level of the performer are equally matched.

Therefore, it would appear to be reasonable to assume that moments of creative insight might be inextricably a product of *flow*. That is, in order to have a moment of creative insight concerning a work of art, or anything else for that matter, one must be absorbed in the object of one's perceptions at a level that significantly challenges one's understanding of that object.

In addition, Jung-Beeman argues that in order for someone to apprehend a work of art with true creative insight, they must not only concentrate on it but also allow their mind to wander to the extent that it begins to focus not just on the details of the particular work but also on the overall, bigger picture the work represents. In other words, a period of mental relaxation is necessary for that crucial *Aha!* moment associated with creative insight to take place.

It is also clear to some who study the matter that insight is something generated by what might be termed intelligence, a product of a universal Mind distinct from one's thinking mind, while knowledge is something that is generated only through the assimilation of facts and information. In fact, according to Krishnamurti, insight is possessed of an energy that sustains itself, and furthermore is capable of seeing the essence of something in a *flash* specifically because it is free of the energy-draining activities of thought.

Naturally, one does not tend to apprehend significant works of art through the logic of rational thought, but rather through moments of immediate creative insight to which those such as Jung-Beeman or Krishnamurti are referring, or through moments of complete absorption toward which Csikszentmihalyi's flow state might lead. Whether it's the complete transcendence of form that reveals the uninhibited expression of the artist in a Jackson Pollack splatter painting, the intense longing for some otherworldly surrender in the slow movement of Antonin Dvorak's New World Symphony, or the expression of that borderline existing somewhere between primal essence and madness in the poems contained in Sylvia Plath's startling *Ariel* collection, it would appear to be rather obvious that one comes into direct touch with these sort of creative dynamics through immediate moments of direct insight, or not at all.

What's more, if this type of immediate personal involvement with a certain work of art that might lead one toward a larger consciousness born of the work's unique dynamics is to take place, it seems certain that this can occur only in moments of direct insight and complete absorption. Attempting to think one's way into the universal truths represented by these special works, and others like them, solely through one's limiting rational thought processes is nothing short of a fool's errand doomed to end in frustration. Apprehending the larger, otherworldly truths that these works might represent can occur only in that moment of direct insight in which one's consciousness is both enriched and expanded into something larger.

Therefore, because we are now living in a new Internet age in which there is increasing evidence that people's minds and brains are being significantly impacted by how they are using their digital devices, it would seem that the question of what effect this new age and its devices might be having on the potential for moments of creative insight, particularly those having to do with the arts and the search for a larger awareness, needs to be thoroughly examined.

In particular, is the sort of distracted awareness that many neuroscientists, cognitive psychologists, and others insist is occurring today in our current digital age going to make it increasingly difficult for people to experience that *Aha!* moment of recognition that is representative of direct insight and creative absorption?

In order to answer this question, we need to turn back toward the issue of attention in relation to the possible effects that people's use of their digital devices might be having upon it. For one thing, how might our attentiveness to and understanding of our natural surroundings be impacted by the interruption machines that our tablets, phones, and PCs often become for us?

One of the great attendees to his natural surroundings, of course, was the visionary nineteenth-century writer Henry David Thoreau, whose attentiveness to all different aspects of the natural world—from specific bird calls and animal sounds to different types of wildflowers to the trembling surface of an icy winter pond to what he saw as the immortal essence of white pine trees in Maine—was nothing short of pristine and otherworldly. And, as many people already know, Thoreau's tendency to completely lose himself in the details of the natural world reached its apex with his journey into the woods around Concord, Massachusetts, where he lived in a cabin at the edge of Walden Pond for two years and wrote about the wild and domestic animal species he came upon in the forests, farms, and wetlands near Concord in his iconic book *Walden*.

Thoreau believed that paradise itself exists all around us in the wild, natural environment of the American continent, where he discovered in the contact between his own body and America's forests, lakes, rivers, mountains, and animals what Robert Pogue Harrison described in his recent article about Thoreau in the *New York Review of Books* as the "hard bottom home" or "reality" that we all crave.

Suffice it to say that Thoreau's attentiveness to the details of his existence was nothing short of an otherworldly vision of sorts. Yet it was the intensity of his attention from which this vision sprang—an intensity existing at the point at which his mental, emotive, and spiritual life became one and the same. Indeed, the fact that he was most likely a lifelong virgin tends to make perfect sense considering that his apprehension of the details of the natural world that he loved could be described as being nothing short of erotic.

When compared to the heightened state of intensity in which Thoreau lived, our own cyber world of digital devices in which many of us now live so thoroughly would appear to be more than a little unreal—a potential barrier between us and the natural world with which Thoreau was able to put himself in touch.

Similarly, the world in which the poet Walt Whitman lived through his own inner life makes the cyber world today in which so many people live seem paltry, stifling, and even narrow-minded. Whitman, as those familiar with his poetry are certainly aware, believed so intensely in the fusion of the body with the mind and the soul that he advocated our thoughts and feelings actually begin with physical sensations.

Because he believed so completely in how our thoughts and emotions represent our body's reactions to our physical environment, Whitman became determined to write poetry that expressed this even though during that time medical science was convinced that our feelings come primarily from our thoughts, while the body was simply along for the ride, so to speak. In fact, Whitman's faith in the holiness of all physical sensations, even that of the orgasm (despite the fact that it shocked people at the time), was something that helped rid the nineteenth- and twentieth-century world of its misguided faith in the mind-body dualism that had existed for centuries.

Whitman's great book of poems, *Leaves of Grass*, is in many ways the literary bookend of Thoreau's *Walden*, with both authors having come to the realization that one's bodily reaction to the details of the physical world is indeed something deeply spiritual that leads toward the realm of an otherworldly connection to the earth and to other people. In fact, Whitman wrote in the opening lines of *Leaves of Grass*, "Every atom belonging to me as good belongs to you."

Similarly, Thoreau wrote a description in *Walden* of the bean field in which he worked, tilling the soil. He wrote of how he watched a nighthawk circle overhead during sunny afternoons, descending at times with a swoop and sound that reminded him of the heavens above being torn open while a seamless coping of the phenomenon of nature manifested itself in the eggs of small imps that had been laid on the bare sand and rocks of some nearby hills.

He observed a pair of hen-hawks circling in the sky above, their alternate soaring and descending being experienced by him as the embodiment of his own thinking mind. And when he unearthed with his hoe some rotten tree stump from which a sluggish salamander emerged, he found himself suddenly transported back to ancient Egypt on the Nile.

Whitman wrote in *Leaves of Grass* of how he saw in his mind's eye the sights and sounds of a child who goes forth into the world every day in the shadows cascading over the roofs of nearby villages at sunset; in the hurrying, tumbling waves and their broken curls slapping against a schooner in the harbor; in the movement of clouds juxtaposed against a motionless maroon-colored sky at sunset; and in hearing at the horizon's edge a sea crow flying amid the fragrance of salt marshes and shore mud.

In order to have the sort of deep, immediate contact with the physical world that both Thoreau and Whitman had, a relationship with their environment that occurred at such a heightened level of awareness that at times it appears to reach toward the infinite, one's sensorial and emotive lives must necessarily exist at a level where there are no barriers, either physical or mental, conscious or unconscious, separating one from the details of the world that one is experiencing. In other words, a pure state of heightened perception in which the observer and the observed are one and the same.

Yet in contradiction to this state of heightened awareness, today's smartphones and other digital devices would appear to be both a physical and an interior barrier separating people from the details of the world that they inhabit. They are an obvious physical barrier simply because of how people spend so much time staring into their plastic screens in lieu of observing the details of the world that is transpiring all around them.

At the same time, they may be a much more significant internal barrier separating people from their world simply by virtue of the fact that as many people begin to accept the more diluted experience that the cyber world provides, instead of the more enriching experiences taking place in the real world, it is easy to see how they might begin to establish a certain unconscious barrier within themselves for how intensely those real world experiences might affect them.

Indeed, much more research needs to be done on this issue of how the digital world is conditioning people toward a more dulled, stifled apprehension of the life that is taking place all around them. Perhaps longitudinal studies need to be developed to examine how the strength of emotive life is being affected in those who spend time staring into the face of their digital devices with a certain amount of regularity.

Certainly, there are already any number of studies being undertaken that examine how a distracted awareness and new forms of Internet addiction are increasingly transpiring in many who spend their time captivated by their phones, tablets, or PCs. At the same time, however, the issue of how our digital age and its devices might be diluting people's inner lives to the point that it becomes extremely difficult for the sort of connection to the details of real-world experience that was part of the inner lives of a Thoreau or a Whitman to exist seems not to be on many people's radar screens.

There have in fact been studies that deal with how during the advent of our current digital age researchers have found a significant drop in empathy that young people tend to have for one another, as well as how they are becoming desensitized to shocking images and events that they have observed online or in the media.

Jennifer Aaker, a professor at the Stanford Graduate School of Business and coauthor of the book *The Dragonfly Effect*, analyzed seventy-two studies performed on nearly 14,000 college students between 1979 and 2009 and found a sharp decline in the trait of empathy over the last ten years, empathy being a trait that requires human touch, face-to-face interactions, and communication through verbal as well as nonverbal cues.

Similarly, in studying the possible decrease in empathy that might be occurring in young people as a result of the shocking images and gruesome videos that regularly occur online in our Internet age, Sara H. Konrath, director of the Interdisciplinary Program on Empathy and Altruism Research at Indiana University, found during the course of a recent study that the self-reported empathy of college students has declined from 1980 to 2015, with a steep drop occurring within the past decade; this report understandably coinciding with a rise in the self-reported narcissism of students found by Jean M. Twenge, a psychologist at San Diego State University.

These studies would appear to point to a stifling of emotional intelligence in young people—such intelligence, according to Travis Bradberry and Jean

Greaves, co-authors of the book *Emotional Intelligence 2.0*, being the ability to recognize and understand emotions in oneself and others. Likewise, Daniel Goleman, author of several books on emotional intelligence, including his immensely popular *Emotional Intelligence*, which brought the subject to the forefront of public awareness in the mid-1990s, believes that the expanding hours spent alone with gadgets and digital tools could lower emotional intelligence due to a lessening of the time young people spend in face-to-face interactions.

While a lack of emotional intelligence and empathy do not necessarily directly represent a dulling of people's inner lives in our current digital age, they may well be symptoms of this alarming development. As people grow desensitized to their own emotions due to time spent apprehending their world through the virtual images that bombard them daily on a plastic screen, their reactions to the world taking place all around them during their daily lives, as well as their connection to the natural world, are bound to be similarly stifled.

Furthermore, as this deadening process continues to occur, there will almost certainly be a concurrent lessening of the capacity for direct insight into great works of art in relation to the possibility of a large awareness, as well as a lessening of direct insight into oneself, other people, and events that occur during the course of one's daily existence as many people grow increasingly removed from the richness and depth that their real-world experiences may be able to offer them.

In addition, the possibility for the sort of complete absorption that is part of Csikszentmihalyi's flow state, that which is necessary for true insight into experiences and events to take place, may likewise be lessened as people's inner lives become increasingly dulled as they jump back and forth between a sea of virtual images on the plastic screens of their digital devices while growing increasingly less able to sink into their own inner experience in relation to the events of their daily lives.

Furthermore, as many people grow less able to surrender to the flow state representative of complete absorption, certain important works of art may become increasingly inaccessible to them. In terms of literature, the great stream-of-consciousness writers like Marcel Proust, Virginia Woolf, Henry Miller, or Jack Kerouac might become more difficult to read simply because it will become increasingly difficult for those whose minds are conditioned by their experience in a cyber world that delivers information and knowledge in increasingly fragmented pieces to become absorbed in the flow of those great authors' writing and to gain insight into what these people might have to tell us.

In addition, what these great writers might be telling us about the nature of our minds, particularly about memory in relation to personal experience, may become lost on many of us, decreasing the possibility that we might have immediate, direct insight into the nature of our own thought processes. For instance, we can learn from reading Woolf's *Mrs. Dalloway* how consciousness itself may be able to move fluidly between one person and another. In addition, as has been alluded to earlier, Marcel Proust has much to teach us about the incomplete nature of memory. Or Kerouac can reveal to us how the mere description of the details of life can without further analysis or explanation be part of a much larger vision of existence.

In other words, great literary artists such as these can help reveal to us the nature of our thinking minds, memory, and consciousness by presenting these things to us directly in the form of the stories they have written. Yet, in order to learn from what they teach us, it is obviously necessary to have the sort of direct insight into the knowledge that they may be imparting by experiencing that *Aha!* moment of creative absorption in which we are able to look without hesitation into the actual dynamics of our own thinking minds and inner lives.

This means that we're not going to be able to put ourselves in touch with what Woolf may have to impart to us concerning consciousness unless we're able to understand in the moment in which we are reading her novel how an omniscient description of events, interior monologues, characters, and even their soliloquies might be mixed together in order to reveal how a common consciousness can flow between different people. That is, if we try to analyze to too great an extent what techniques Woolf is employing with her writing, rather than absorbing them directly, we can easily miss what she is saying to us concerning how consciousness is something fluid that can move from one person to another so effortlessly.

Likewise, if we're able to become absorbed in Proust's stream-of-consciousness writing about the events of his youth that take place in his *Remembrance of Things Past* to the point that we allow its flow to carry us along in the stream, without impeding this flow by attempting to analyze plot, character, themes, and so on (as we would tend to do with a number of other novels), we stand a much better chance of apprehending what he may have been trying to say to us about the illusory nature of memory.

Or if we're unable to read Kerouac's *The Subterraneans*, a book about a failed interracial love affair in 1950s San Francisco, without surrendering to the orgasmic intensity of the book, one that is similar to the bebop jazz of Charley Parker and other musicians who influenced Kerouac so thoroughly at the time, we will likewise be unable to experience it as the long jazz poem that it actually is. Consequently, we'll be left unable to experience that *Aha!* moment in which we realize how music and writing can emanate from the same rhythms of life.

Ultimately, creative absorption, rather than intellectual analysis, is what makes great works of art accessible to us in a manner in which we're able to put ourselves in touch with a larger reality toward which they are potentially leading. Yet, at the same time, two genuine impediments to these absorbing moments of immediate creative insight are a fragmented, interrupted awareness and a diluted inner life.

So if it becomes clearer over time, as one imagines it might, that our digital world and how people are using their digital devices are responsible for both of these impediments, then it would appear that an obvious, direct connection might be established between our digital world, our growing incapacity to put ourselves fully in touch with great works of art, and the possibility of those great works leading us to a larger, more expansive awareness.

Also, ultimately if someone is pursuing a more expansive consciousness, one that leads outward from an insightful understanding of the dynamics of one's thinking mind, that person will only be able to accomplish that if he or she is doing so through the power of direct insight, this being so because one simply cannot think one's way into comprehending how the processes of thought and memory take place, in addition to understanding just how limiting they can be, without the power of direct insight.

Furthermore, if one has been able to apply this sort of direct insight to the apprehension of great works of art, then it would appear to be so much easier to apply it to understanding the nature of consciousness itself. Thought, worry, and the seeking of solutions are processes of the mind; yet, because the mind itself is the maker of the problems, it can't possibly resolve them. One can only do so through direct insight into how the mind and thought hold people captive in such a circular fashion.

It requires a certain subtlety of mind that few people possess—an intuitive quality that allows one to temporarily stand outside his or her own mind without beginning to lose it. It is likewise a quality that involves an intense focus and an enriched inner life that is sensitive to how the particulars of one's immediate environment might be affecting him or her.

As has been elucidated earlier in this work, both of those qualities are now under assault by the fragmented awareness being engendered in people by the nature of the Internet, which doles out information in fragmented pieces, and by the virtual objects on one's plastic screen to which so many people currently surrender in lieu of placing themselves in touch with people, activities, and situations in real time and space.

Yet without a highly focused span of attention, and without a highly sensitive emotive life, this journey into the nature of one's mind in search of some greater awareness is not only a futile enterprise but also a potentially dangerous undertaking in which, if one does not have his wits fully about him, he can find himself trapped in a maddening nowhere land existing midway between rational thought and the world of the limitless without a genuine road map available for his return.

Most people will never embark on such a journey, or even have any real interest in doing so. Yet that doesn't mean that it is not still of critical importance that at least some people have the mental resources necessary to successfully undertake it. And even though this particular concern is still far from the vast majority of people's minds in relation to the use of their smartphones, tablets, or PCs, to which they are becoming increasingly addicted, for those of us who do have such an interest, the effects on our minds and physiological brains by how we might be using our digital devices is something about which we need to be vitally concerned.

There is also the issue of how people's conceptions of time and space might be adversely affected in our digital age, and what effect this might have on their search for an expansive awareness. If it is true, as it may well be, that the time and space that used to exist comfortably between and within all of us are being contracted at an increasingly rapid rate by the speed at which information travels in the Internet age, then it seems possible that this might have a profound effect on the time and space needed to comfortably navigate the pathways of one's thinking mind in order to approach a larger reality that might exist beyond the boundaries of rational thought.

That is, the center, the *me* that we inhabit daily, may grow increasingly constricted as our attention spans grow shorter, our inner lives grow more diluted, and the potential chemical addictions in our brains engendered by how we're using digital technologies become more solidified. And as the constriction of this center continues to take place, it will likewise become increasingly difficult to peek over its edge in search of a potentially limitless reality.

Our use of digital devices in the Internet age may well be constricting both the space within us and the psychological time in which we pursue the events of our lives, with these dynamics tending to have a profound effect on our inner lives. Yet how this might be happening needs to be explained in a certain amount of detail. So this is where we will turn our attention next— toward the potential effects on psychological space and time wrought by our current digital age.

Chapter Nine

Space and Time in the Digital World

As late as three thousand years ago, prehistoric people still did not distinguish in their minds between their external environment and themselves. As Julian Jaynes, the late psychologist who studied human consciousness, wrote about in his book *The Origin of Consciousness in the Breakdown of the Bicameral Mind*, they had no "I" consciousness that would distinguish them from the particulars of their surroundings with which they had to deal in order to stay alive on a daily basis.

Then, according to Jaynes, our ancestors suddenly became aware of themselves as individual beings who could exert a measure of control in dealing with their world, much as a newborn baby realizes it can do when it begins to use its hands to grasp its surroundings. As this separation of self from world progressed, and people became increasingly able to use tools to manipulate their environment, and as they developed both spoken and written language, over time humans became increasingly aware of the thoughts inside their minds and of the space inside them as a separate entity.

Eventually, as people began to leave behind their superstitions concerning some divine being who controlled their lives from some larger reality, religious seekers and other brave souls began to attempt to discover whether there was a way to fuse the space within them and the space in which they lived as a unitary consciousness in which all became one. A result of this experiment was the origination of the ancient religions of the East, such as Buddhism, Hinduism, or Taoism, which emphasized humanity's quest to become psychologically united not only with the world in which they live but also with the entire universe.

Many years later, working from the other side of the spectrum, scientists like Einstein began to discover that people had a decided relation to the physical space surrounding them, rather than just living in it. That is, the planet on which they lived and the sun around which it orbited could actually curve the fabric of universal space in a manner that affected the movement of bodies through that space. Consequently, at the same time that it became increasingly apparent to the scientific world how malleable the fabric of universal space might be, those who were concerned with man's spiritual and psychological development began to likewise think about the potential malleability of inner space—how it might be shaped by things like thought or one's contact with other human beings.

Eventually, metaphysical seekers like Krishnamurti began to not only seek a limitless space that might exist outside the boundaries of rational thought but also consider possible pathways through one's own inner space for reaching that expansive reality. As part of that search, they began to increasingly consider the potentially illusory nature of the individual self, a center or *me*—an entity that might simply be a construction of the thinking mind. In addition, those seekers and psychologists such as R. D. Laing, who was likewise studying the dynamics of the space inside people in relation to their environment, began to consider just how deeply the space within people might be affected by the world in which they live—that is, just how constricted or expansive it might become according to how conditioned someone is by their personal experiences with other people or with society.

As almost everyone already knows, the late physicist Stephen Hawking was involved in studying black holes in space for most of his professional life, learning how an extreme amount of matter or the extreme density of matter present in the gravitational force of a dying star as it collapses in upon itself can warp the surrounding space until it too collapses to a point of infinite density known as a singularity. Conversely, Hawking and others have studied how the Big Bang at the time of the birth of the universe originated an expansion of universal space that various instruments employed by physicists tell us is still going on to this very day.

Because it would appear to make sense to imagine that the dynamics of space might operate in the same manner when applied to either universal or psychological space, it seems logical to conclude that the space within us in relation to the space that surrounds us may likewise be continually in the process of either contracting or expanding.

If it contracts, we become more closed in upon ourselves as we become more neurotic; if it expands, we become more integrated, whole, and in touch with other people and with the world in which we live. Ultimately, if one is able to take the inner voyage far enough, the space within oneself and the space in which one lives become one and the same.

Given this idea that universal and psychological space operate in the same manner, the question in relation to this particular work becomes one of what effect our Internet age and our use of digital devices might have on either the contraction or the expansion of psychological space. To put a finer point on the matter, is the manner in which we use our devices in this new age we have entered inevitably causing the space within us to constrict due to the effects that our use of digital technologies might be having on our minds, brains, and inner lives?

A recent Pew Research Center survey found that 67 percent of cell phone owners find themselves continually checking their phones even when they're not ringing or vibrating just to see whether anyone is trying to contact them. This modern-day form of addiction in which people are psychologically chained to their digital devices is obviously something that is not good for developing a focused attention span, as well as avoiding a fragmented, interrupted one. Yet an even more potentially dangerous consequence may be how this subservience to the digital world might be affecting people's inner space.

Could there in fact be a significant dynamic relationship between a fragmented, continually distracted mind and an increasing constriction of the space within one? Or, to put it another way, as people's attention spans grow shorter and more easily interrupted as a result of how they are using their digital devices, are the boundaries of their self, or center, beginning to likewise close more tightly around them in reaction to this interrupted awareness?

R. D. Laing, in describing how the schizoid condition develops within people, writes in *The Divided Self* of how a self develops that feels as if it is outside all experience and activity as it increasingly becomes an inner vacuum where everything is there (outside) while nothing is here (inside).

Moreover, the constant dread of being overwhelmed and engulfed by the outside world is mitigated by the need to keep the world at bay even as that person, more than anything, longs for participation in that world. As much as anything, Laing's description of this constriction of inner space would appear to be a chillingly accurate picture of an inner world that has grown increasingly narrowed simply because it lacks full participation in the activities of the external world.

Therefore, what might an abbreviated, continually interrupted attention span, one that those who have studied the matter have found is occurring as a result of how people are using their digital devices, have to do with the creation of this type of personal inner vacuum? The answer to that question may lie in looking at how the degree to which people are able to completely inhabit their experiences might have a decided effect on how fully they are able to make contact with their world, rather than remain isolated from it to the point that their inner life begins to grow empty.

One of the most important personal characteristics that allows people to fully sink into and absorb their experience is, of course, a lack of anxiety. The more relaxed people are, the more fully focused and attentive to what is occurring inside them they become as they interact with their environment. Unfortunately, one of the consequences of people jumping back and forth on their phones and computers between websites, text messages, and the like is that this process tends to create a type of self-induced permanently anxious state in which people become habituated to anxiously seeking the next bit of virtual information, fearing that they might be missing something important.

In a recent study undertaken in Dr. Larry Rosen's lab at California State University, Dominguez Hills, and spearheaded by Dr. Nancy Cheever, the role that technology use—or lack of it—has on anxiety was investigated. A group of college students was brought into a lecture hall and told to turn off their phones and store them under their seat while simply doing nothing. Another group, while also simply doing nothing, had their smartphones taken away from them, being told that they would be given back with a claim check for retrieval. Then, minutes later, and twice more, both groups of students took a paper and pencil measure of anxiety.

What the researchers found, surprisingly, was that although they anticipated that the anxiety level of the students whose phones were taken away would be significantly higher than the students who merely placed them out of sight, the anxiety levels for both groups turned out to be relatively the same. That is, the anxiety level of students who merely put their phones out of sight was just as high as those who had them physically removed.

What this obviously suggests is that one can be psychologically addicted to one's digital devices even when they are not in one's physical presence, which means that the anxiety generated by their use has now become internal. In other words, that same level of anxiety that occurs when one continually needs to search webpages or look for text messages or emails has now become a permanent part of one's psyche or emotive life.

As a response to this situation, the same distracted, interrupted awareness being wrought by one's smartphone or PC, it would seem, tends to occur intrinsically inside people regardless of whether they are in fact using those devices. Then, in a perpetual cycle, this same internally conditioned interrupted awareness leads toward further anxiety, and on and on, until someone's level of interior anxiety reaches the point that they are prevented from sinking fully into the particulars of their own experience as completely as they otherwise might. Yet, at the same time, because they appear to themselves to be just as focused and attentive while jumping around on their digital devices, it becomes harder for those people to realize the permanently anxious, fragmented awareness that is being conditioned into them in the world of real time and space.

In fact, one has to wonder whether, years from now, if people begin trying to release themselves from their digital addiction by staying away from their devices as much as possible, will they even be able to recognize the hazardous changes to their awareness and attention spans that the cyber world has wrought simply because the fragmented, distracted awareness that has been conditioned into them by the new Internet age has become the new normal?

A significant hazardous change that might be occurring to people's inner lives in our Internet age, one that is just as dangerous as a fragmented awareness and an unfocused attention, is the constriction of inner space that might occur within them as they are less able to remain attentive to and absorbed by their experience of their external surroundings as they grow more anxious. That is, will people lose a significant amount of personal depth and become shallower people because of this development?

And will they become more neurotic and less emotively healthy as a result of this continuing inner constriction? Or will they eventually not even notice that these deleterious changes are occurring simply because they have become so inured to a new, digital mindset?

One thing that is already proving to be troubling in this regard is how communities of people are being replaced by isolated communication between people who either barely know one another or don't know each other at all. Social critic Joe Lockard warns that to accept only communication in place of a community's manifold functions is to sell our faith in community vastly short while leading people to evade offline or "real world" difficulties, problems, and social issues.

An early critic of the Internet, astronomer, author, and teacher Clifford Stoll, raised fears in his book *Silicon Snake Oil: Second Thoughts on the Information Highway* that genuine and deep connections between people are being replaced with shallow and inadequate substitutes. Later critics, such as Nancy K. Baym in her book *Personal Connections in the Digital Age*, refer to the specter of people isolated indoors who are substituting a "floating world" of connection for meaningful contact with neighbors.

In a 2015 article in *The Guardian*, "The Future of Loneliness," British writer and cultural critic Olivia Laing, author of the recent book *The Lonely City*, writes about how the cure for loneliness is the act of being seen by other people as the person that one actually is. That is, as she puts it, when one is lonely, one longs to be witnessed by others. Yet, at the same time, according to research carried out over the past decade at the University of Chicago, the lonely person becomes hyper-alert to rejection.

So, Laing goes on to say, the Internet can exercise a certain seductive charm for someone who is lonely and isolated simply because behind a computer screen the lonely person has control. That is, they can reach out to others, safe from the humiliation of face-to-face rejection. Of course, the problem with this is that because online communication is not intimacy or true friendship, the lonely person can grow even more isolated in their mode of self-protection as the unhealthy cycle continues.

The significantly greater dependence on isolated communication that is occurring these days as people increasingly use their digital devices to communicate with one another while eschewing face-to-face, more personal communication may in fact be evidence that people are beginning to significantly dispense with their need for community in accepting the isolated communication that is increasingly becoming a hallmark of our digital age. Correspondingly, if this is indeed true, will this new floating world of isolated communication lead toward a constriction of the space within people as they grow ever more closed in upon themselves?

If the anxiety in people brought on by a more fragmented, interrupted digital awareness increases as they become ever more habituated to jumping between bits of information on the Internet, and if as a reaction to this anxiety (in addition to being one of its primary causes) isolated communication in our digital world—that in which people feel more protected and in control—continues to increase, the personal isolation that leads inevitably to more constricted, barren inner lives is almost certain to increasingly become a significant part of people's psyches.

Yet in order to look at this potential alarming trend more closely, the exact relationship between the inner world and consciousness in relation to space and time might need to be investigated more acutely.

The inner voyage is a journey in which the inner world and outer reality begin to merge with one another, a journey in which one begins to realize that the idea of *me* might potentially be an illusory product of our thinking minds. Then, as one's consciousness begins to merge with the outer world, *me* is no longer such an intrinsic barrier to that occurring as the space within one begins to move toward the limitless. It is likewise a journey in which one might begin to realize that the movements of thought and time are one and the same.

Therefore, the question becomes one of considering whether the specific effects of our digital devices on our minds and brains might affect them in such a way that the movement toward this voyage of self-discovery involving space and time is inevitably impeded. How might the dynamics of space and time be altered in the digital mind? Might space be constricted and time compressed in a manner that makes the journey toward a more expansive consciousness increasingly difficult to achieve?

As was mentioned earlier, one creates a mapping of the space that one inhabits in the hippocampus region of the brain, a picture of one's world that allows a person to place his or her life experiences within their proper context. In this regard, it is very much a picture of not only the world that one navigates on a daily basis but also the internal space within one by which one is able to internalize that navigation. And of course, as has been elucidated earlier, it is highly dependent upon the brain's ability to engender and maintain long-term memories.

Neuroscientists like Eric Kandel have known for some time now that the neurotransmitter serotonin plays a key role in the growth of synaptic terminals that allow for the creation and perpetuation of long-term memories. At the same time, serotonin has an inverse relationship with the neurotransmitter dopamine. More of one tends to mean less of the other, and vice versa.

In fact, neuroscientists have said that serotonin and dopamine can be thought of as being two different glasses of milk. Together the two glasses take up 100 units of fluid, with each glass taking 50 percent of the total. So, in order to maintain a hundred units of fluid, you must borrow from one of the hypothetical glasses in order to fill the other. Furthermore, if our lives and brain activity are to remain balanced, there must be relatively fifty units in the dopamine glass and fifty units in the serotonin glass. If, however, they become out of balance, the more likely it is that our brain activity will be affected.

In addition, as was likewise discussed earlier, high levels of dopamine have been shown to be present in those who are subject to digital addiction, compulsively spending time with their smartphones, tablets, or PCs.

So the question seemingly needs to be asked with regard to Internet addiction, the chemical functioning of the brain, and the search for an expansive consciousness: Does an overabundance of dopamine in the brain brought on by an excessive use of one's digital devices negatively affect the production of serotonin and consequently the brain's ability to produce the long-term memories that are essential to its capacity to produce an accurate cognitive mapping of one's world in the brain's hippocampus region?

And if that is indeed the case, what effect might this diminished capacity of one's brain to produce an accurate picture of both the inner and the outer space that one traverses daily have on the search for an expansive awareness?

In Carlos Castaneda's series of books, the Yaqui Indian spiritual teacher Don Juan used the vast space of the Mexican desert to assist Carlos in merging this space with the potentially vast space within him. Einstein used the malleability of the fabric of space to prove that space and time are one and the same. Lao Tzu described the Tao as a well that is used but never used up—an eternal void filled with infinite possibilities.

Krishnamurti often said that when there is no center and you look at the details of the world, there is vast, immeasurable space. Alan Watts asked the question, "Where do I begin and end in space?" And Aldous Huxley found on his journey into consciousness with the drug mescaline that space was still there, but it had lost its predominance, his mind being primarily concerned not with measures and locations but with, as he put it, being and meaning.

Obviously, how one apprehends both the space within oneself and the space surrounding one is a key component to seeking a larger consciousness. Yet what if one's internal space, one's cognitive or spatial map, has been compromised by long-term memories that have been made either unclear or entirely inaccessible due to a distracted awareness and an information overload in the digital world that make it increasingly difficult for short-term memories to be converted into long-term ones?

In this respect, one would assume that the capacity to navigate the details of one's outer world by internalizing them within their proper context and relation to one another might well be the same process by which one navigates the territory of inner space. That is to say, examining the structure of one's thinking mind, the potential illusory nature of memory in relation to thought, and the conditioning imposed upon one by his or her social environment might well be similar in nature to how one moves through the physical world in which one lives without getting lost while managing the specifics of one occupation, or correctly absorbing the details of a book one is reading in their proper order.

However, if one's ability to attend is being compromised by things like an obsessive use of one's smartphone, compulsive postings on social media, or the constant need to text message, things for which there is increasing evidence can lead to an attention deficit, then it seems almost inevitable that this lack of attention will make it more difficult to clearly examine inner dynamics like the limitations of thought and memory in the same way that a lack of attention might necessarily affect one's capacity to form a clear cognitive mapping of the external world that one traverses daily.

Navigating the space within oneself has very much to do with examining the potential limitations of the thinking mind, learning how thought may be useful and how it can become a potential barrier to clearly perceiving the world that one inhabits. Anyone who has spent a significant amount of time following his or her thoughts to a point of completion, while at the same time observing from a place outside of them, surely already knows, or else has a strong inclination about this. That is, they realize that this is a different type of mental activity from that to which we have become accustomed during the normal course of our daily lives. As much as anything, it involves the sort of insightful thinking that is both intuitive and three dimensional.

Stepping outside one's thinking mind in order to carefully examine not only the limitations of thought but also how thought can be responsible for the illusory nature of memory, needless to say, is an activity that requires an extraordinary degree of attention. Yet this is what the exploration of inner space is all about—examining the potential barriers that keep us imprisoned within our own minds, those that cause us to constantly run around in circles without ever touching down inside that still mind which might allow the limitless to enter its spaces.

Ultimately, the quiet mind that might allow the limitless to enter because one's thinking mind is no longer habitually (if indirectly) blocking its appearance is at the root of an expansive consciousness. Likewise, this concept is also at the heart of the ultimate danger that our Internet age, and our obsessive use of digital devices, may be inflicting upon us, even as we fail to realize that is what is occurring.

The possibility of a still mind is being consistently abnegated in so many different ways by the distracted, jumpy, unfocused awareness that is increasingly causing many people to be incapable of following an extended piece of writing or prevent themselves from habitually jumping around their phones or PCs within a world of multitasking, much less being attentive enough to actually step outside of and observe the dynamics of thought in relation to their thinking minds.

There is also something else. In Hermann Hesse's iconic novel *Siddartha*, the title character tells his old friend Govinda, who has spent a lifetime searching for *nirvana*, how important it is to love the world as it is and not try to compare it with some other imaginary world. Yet doing that, it would seem, requires an extreme attentiveness to the details of the world in which one lives. Loving the world in all its detail means that one is constantly attentive.

If people are engendering a distracted, jumpy awareness within themselves, something to which they become increasingly habituated due to their use of digital technology and social media, that quality of attentiveness will surely be diminished in people over time. As a result, they might never be able to sink fully into the potentially exquisite fabric of their natural or human environments.

At the same time, as people grow increasingly habituated to a distracted awareness as a result of how they are using their smartphones and PCs, they are becoming less free, increasingly controlled by powerful search engines with their algorithms in ways of which most of us are probably not even aware.

Our modern age, which presented the world with the possibility of a larger intelligence, began, to a certain extent, in the sidewalk cafes of post–World War II Paris, where great writers such as Jean-Paul Sartre, Albert Camus, and Simone de Beauvoir wrote of how absolute freedom is a basic existential condition that people only have to grab for themselves and that one's personal chains are really just a failure to realize this essential nature of existence.

Now, unfortunately, during the advent of our new digital age during the past thirty or so years, that freedom is being imperiled by a new type of conditioning brought about by a powerful cyber world where the network of our own thoughts, that for which we should always possess genuine ownership, are slowly but surely melding with the digital networks through which we increasingly receive our information, networks controlled by those who desire to make money from us by selling us their advertising and services.

In the end, the possibility of consciousness expansion begins with freeing oneself from his or her conditioning. Yet if we're increasingly unaware of exactly how we're being conditioned by a virtual world that is never fully a part of the real one, that goal becomes ever more impossible to achieve. With that idea in mind, it would appear to be more than a little evident that we take time to examine next how our basic existential freedom might be imperiled by the virtual world inside our computers and phones.

Chapter Ten

The Meaning of Freedom in the Digital Age

Personal freedom has always involved the idea of a lack of external barriers, or at least the ability to transcend them. If one is trapped by the social or economic circumstances in which one is forced to live, then one can take action against them by developing the educational or personal qualifications that will allow him or her to leave them or else ignoring those inhibiting circumstances by living a life that allows one to block them from view. Likewise, if one is trapped inside the parameters of an unhealthy personal relationship, then one can either leave it or simply accept it while, at the same time, distancing oneself mentally or emotionally from it.

Of course, there are all sorts of ways, either directly or indirectly, of escaping these situations. Yet now, it would seem, we may be living in an Internet age in which the loss of our personal freedom may not be so obvious, having become more indirect and psychological in nature. That is, we are being conditioned by powerful algorithms and coding inside our digital devices in ways in which our psychological freedom may be under assault even before we realize that that is what is occurring.

When we enter the digital world through the use of our phones, PCs, or tablets, we are also entering unawares the sort of ultimate existential dilemma that has a profound effect on our personal freedom as we become both observer and observed. In a manner similar to how Simone de Beauvoir, Jean-Paul Sarte's lifelong friend and lover, wrote that women face a certain existential bind by having to develop their own viewpoint toward their life and the world at the same time that they have become the viewpoint of others, we are consistently being observed through the digital mirror even as we gaze at our own reflection.

The digital memories inside powerful search engines in our phones and computers often know where we'll be navigating next in cyberspace often before we even do. Anyone who has ever searched Amazon or begun receiving spam emails from out of the blue based on their personal search history knows this fact all too well. In fact, the algorithms of Google and other search engines are now not only able to feed us information they have gathered about us but also direct us to where we should travel next in cyberspace even before we have decided to do that ourselves simply by catching our eye with what they already know we may want to see next based on where we have previously traveled.

Furthermore, this is a fundamental difference from the degree to which various other technologies such as television might have manipulated us in the past. The difference is that while television allows advertisers to push their products at us more effectively by placing particular ads with programs that they know certain groups of people will be watching, or particularly in today's TV milieu, affect the flow of political discourse by hooking people on the personalities or programs of certain TV networks, the Internet is becoming ever more not so much a seduction into a particular reality, like television is, but the reality itself by which we connect ourselves to the outside world that surrounds us.

That is, there is a profound difference between the sort of indirect conditioning to which we're subjected by television or by other social forces or people who are influential in our lives, and the more direct type of conditioning done to us by a cyber world that literally programs us to think, react, and even remember along certain digital pathways inside our phones and computers—a form of conditioning that is much more subtle, dangerous, and less obvious than more personal, socially familiar forms.

One major difference, of course, is that the neural pathways in our brains that direct our thinking minds were formerly only the product of long-term memories created by our personal experiences. That is, it was our own natural memories that created those pathways based on those experiences. Now, however, that we are increasingly outsourcing our working memories to Google and other powerful search engines by obsessively gravitating to them for information, rather than trying to pull that information out of our own natural memories, those same neural pathways are being controlled and directed from the outside, so to speak. That is, they are being determined and controlled by virtual algorithms and computer codes that are entirely non-organic, compared to our entirely organic brains.

And so, although it may be at first difficult to recognize the difference between these two types of memory as we go about habitually retrieving information and knowledge on our phones and PCs, the difference is in fact profound, particularly in terms of the effect that virtual technologies, and how we're using them to outsource our memories, is having on the living networks of thought within our minds and brains.

When our working memories are controlled externally, as they are whenever we go to Google or some other search engine in order to retrieve information that we may not remember, or to which we may not have immediate access, those same neural pathways in our brain that we might formerly have traversed to retrieve the same information more naturally, because they are no longer being used, might inevitably begin to calcify. In other words, what keeps those pathways alive and open is our continual use of them. And when that is no longer occurring, will our long-term memories be in danger of drying up due to lack of use?

In a 2011 study, psychologists and researchers Betsy Sparrow of Columbia University, Jenny Liu of the University of Wisconsin–Madison, and Daniel M. Wegner of Harvard University tested how Internet use might affect memory—that is, how information stored in an external source, such as a digital search engine, might render individuals less likely to store information in their own memory. What they found was that when the subjects they studied expected to have future access to information, they were less likely to remember the specific information, although they were more likely to remember where to find it.

According to the psychologists, in the article they wrote on their study, "Google Effects on Memory: Cognitive Consequences of Having Information at Our Fingertips," their research indicated that once information has been accessed by someone from a search engine or digital database, their internal coding increased for where the information is to be found rather than for the information itself. This would appear to indicate from their study that in our newfound digital world we may be losing access to information stored in our long-term memories even as we become more proficient at where to find it in cyberspace.

That is to say, the increase in our capacity to track down knowledge, facts, and information may be causing us to lose the capacity to store that same information within ourselves. And if this is indeed the case, could this mean that we're becoming less able to internalize the world in which we live? In so doing, becoming less able to come to grips with our own social conditioning as we grow less aware of exactly how our world has conditioned us?

Our inner lives are very much dependent on clearly understanding the dynamics of our external environment, and how we are conditioned by them. If we are to move deeper inside ourselves toward a quiet mind that might lead toward a limitless reality beyond that external world because we have stopped following our thoughts into endless loops and dead-end corners, we must first fully comprehend how our own internal reality is largely synonymous with that of our external world, the first being continually conditioned in us by the second.

Krishnamurti often said, "You are the world," meaning that what we assume to be our autonomous selves are almost entirely a product of our own conditioning by the world in which we live. How we think, how we perceive our own experiences, and how we relate to other people are the result of the very same conditioning to which everyone on the planet is subjected. And if one is to undergo the task of uncovering what one's true self really is, then one must first be aware of all the ways in which one is conditioned.

Yet, at the same time, there has never been a more imposing tool or technological advance designed to inevitably block us from uncovering that conditioning than the Internet, along with all the digital tools that give one access to it.

Now, however, compared to previous technological advances that ended up conditioning people in terms of how they perceived the world, such as television, the digital age is conditioning us in terms of how we think and how we use knowledge and information to learn. Rather than merely conditioning us to perceive and relate to our world in certain habitual ways, the Internet may be actually conditioning the networks of thought inside our minds and brains.

In other words, as we search for information on the Web, following one link to another, or look for possible connections on social media, the once natural pathways of our thoughts and the algorithms that control whatever site we are using are inevitably becoming one and the same simply because we are increasingly surrendering the networks of our thinking minds to the powerful digital pathways inside our computers and phones as they guide us through the digital thicket of information that we mistakenly believe we are freely pursuing.

When we attempt to pull knowledge or information from our actual working memory, we have not given up free will in how we access it. We can backtrack within our memories and follow related information that might lead us toward it. We can investigate other relevant information that might clarify our search, or we can communicate with friends or acquaintances who might assist us. That is, we are still in the driver's seat in directing our working memories and cognitive networks.

However, when we use Google or some other search engine to access the information, we are now very much at the mercy of the virtual links inside whatever digital device we are employing. We can still decide which link we will follow, but the domain in which our search takes place has become extremely limited by whatever algorithms or coding the particular search engine is employing to lead us to the information. That is, the field of inquiry has now become more predetermined as it grows less organic and open-ended.

At the same time, the neuronal networks within our physiological brains are becoming heavily conditioned by the virtual pathways inside our digital devices. As we mistakenly believe that we are exerting free will in employing the technology of the Internet to access the particulars of our world more easily and completely, our minds are being conditioned not only to follow particular pathways to certain information and knowledge but also in terms of how to use our working memories to learn and gain knowledge.

The process of learning involves the use of both implicit and explicit memory. Implicit memory involves the storage of information in the brain that does not require conscious attention for recall. For instance, to use two rather basic examples, once you learn how to ride a bike or write your name, you then do so automatically without having to think about the series of steps the task requires. Explicit memories, by contrast, are long-term memories that involve the storage of information about people, places, or things that require conscious attention to be recalled. For example, a scientist performing a complex experiment in his lab that he has done before will most likely still have to walk himself through the specific steps it involves in words or thoughts.

Often, when we use our working memories to focus our attention on some complex task that we might employ to learn something new, or to recall information that we want to use to seek new knowledge, we are using both our implicit and our explicit memories. That is, certain information, knowledge, and skills may have already become habituated within our brains to the point that we don't have to recall them by putting them into words in order to use them. At the same time, we may need to approach other information, knowledge, and skills logically and sequentially through our long-term memories.

What is critical to this process is that we experience it as emanating from ourselves—from our own working memories, habits, and networks of thought that we have developed over time through our experiences, and that we use whenever we learn something. That is, we are using memories and processes that have been previously stored within us to access new information or to gain new knowledge.

Yet as soon as the Internet and our digital devices become part of the natural process of learning, something quite different occurs. We begin to increasingly experience the synthesis of memory and learning as something that exists outside of us, external to our natural capacity to learn. As links appear almost magically on the plastic screen in front of us in order to guide us toward where we might go next in our search for new knowledge by narrowing the field of information that we might employ, we are now following virtual learning paths that originate entirely outside of us, rather than within our own long-term memories and networks of thought.

Then, as we employ those external pathways to access knowledge and information, those that exist entirely outside our own pathways of thought and memory, there is the significant danger that those external paths begin to increasingly control our own internal ones to the point that our apprehension of the world, and of learning itself, become conditioned disembodied processes that are not truly our own.

In addition, our own internal space, that which is integrally related to the spatial mapping of our world through our long-term memories, might likewise become something that is increasingly conditioned by, as well as becoming dangerously synonymous with the virtual world that we employ to seek knowledge and information.

According to a 2016 article in *Wired* by Cade Metz, Google is now already developing what are called *deep neural networks*, networks of hardware and software that approximate the web of neurons in the human brain. By employing this approach, known as deep learning, these digital networks can analyze vast amounts of digital data in order to learn all sorts of useful tasks, such as identifying photos, recognizing commands spoken into a smartphone, or responding to Internet search queries.

In some cases, they can learn a task so well that they can actually outperform humans. The article then goes on to mention how deep learning is now rapidly reinventing many of the Web's popular social media sites, like Facebook or Twitter, as well as reinventing Google Search.

If in fact our own neural networks in our brains are being used to create digital ones that become even more efficient, then how might this affect how effectively virtual networks can increasingly control our own neural networks? In other words, if the digital networks in people's computers and phones become increasingly based on how their own neural networks take in knowledge, information, and learn, won't it then become much easier for those digital networks to control, condition, and direct how our own minds and brains operate?

As a result, it is easy to see how it can become ever more difficult to apprehend our own conditioning by the world in which we live simply because we are now less in control of both our own natural learning paths and our own interior life. Consequently, a possible internal voyage on which we might embark in search of the true nature of self becomes much more muddied and more difficult to pursue as we grow ever more oblivious to just how our worldview and even our own processes of thought, memory, and learning have become so heavily conditioned.

Once again, critical to such an interior voyage may be the realization of the possible illusion of the individual self, the *me*, something that is the product of thought, and of our own particular conditioning. And this can only take place when one realizes that one's inner and outer worlds are often very much one and the same due to the extent to which we are so thoroughly conditioned by the world in which we live.

Yet if our very own networks of thought, those which we might follow in order to attempt to achieve this startling awareness, are themselves being conditioned by the algorithms and links inside our computers and phones, then the possibility of such an interior voyage, it would seem, becomes exponentially more difficult to pursue. In addition, because our own thought processes, those we might use to guide us on this voyage, are now being conditioned by not only the real but also the virtual world in which we live, the task of developing a larger intelligence grows even more difficult.

Alan Watts wrote of how we should learn to allow ourselves to flow with the great stream of life, and to not produce conflict in ourselves by attempting to *fix* the world when it is we ourselves who *are* that very world. Yet if our own interior lives and thought processes are being increasingly conditioned by a fixed virtual world that we inhabit on a daily basis, then one wonders how we will ever be able to maintain the mental and emotive flexibility to follow this natural stream of existence in search of something larger. Furthermore, will we even be free enough within ourselves to do so?

As much as critics of the Internet, our use of digital devices, and the cyber world itself are now focusing on such things as the distracted awareness that is being created in us or how we are being manipulated by powerful digital platforms who are using our digital fixation to sell us more advertising, two entirely valid and significant concerns, what might be most at stake in this new digital age in which we now find ourselves is our personal, psychological freedom.

Once our own networks of thought become increasingly assimilated by the digital pathways inside our phones and PCs, we may well increasingly lose our capacity to apprehend our own conditioning by the world in which we live, and to remain free enough to avoid it. Furthermore, since the Internet is now the primary means by which people conduct business with each other, or even in many cases establish personal relationships, this sort of pervasive conditioning and loss of psychological freedom will become increasingly impossible to avoid.

For instance, the possible routes for success within a certain field of professional endeavor may become increasingly predetermined by powerful algorithms inside one's PC that more and more people will tend to follow in order to outdo one another in the pursuit of advancing quickly within their chosen profession. In point of fact, this is already occurring in non-digital ways as standard guidelines for advancement in one's chosen field have become indirectly a part of any number of reality TV shows having to do with the development of a particular artistic talent, how to sell real estate, become a better cook, or proceed as an entrepreneur in the business world.

Soon, unfortunately, those standard guidelines for success may well become codified within the digital world through powerful search engines or social media platforms as people become less creative and freewheeling in their thinking in seeking professional success when the temptation to follow certain paths or advice provided on enticing links found on the Internet make the search for professional fulfillment so much easier to pursue.

As a result, the open-ended, creative networks of thought that people may have pursued in the past through the process of trial and error will instead become predetermined by the digital networks born of preconceived algorithms and coding. Then, as this sort of predetermined thinking conditioned into people by their need for easy answers for success becomes ever more prevalent, it will increasingly become part of more closed-minded psychological thought processes that leave people less free even as they're not aware that this is occurring.

Even personal relationships are now being codified in this same manner on social networking sites like Facebook or Instagram as positive experiences with another person have become part of receiving a "like" or some short comment one has posted affirming what someone else has just said online.

As a result of this, there is the very real danger that one's potential personal interactions with others in the real world may increasingly become a product of this same automatic agreement rather than through spirited discussion as the digital *like* button becomes ever more a conditioned part of our psyches. As a potential consequence of this, we may feel increasingly less free to express our actual opinions to friends or acquaintances.

At the same time, as Susan Greenfield has written about in *Mind Change*, excessive Internet use can lead toward a decreased ability to communicate effectively with others simply because if someone is communicating largely with others in the digital world, he or she might lose the ability to interpret actual facial expressions, those which are obviously integral to communicating more deeply with another person.

In one study that Greenfield references, experimenters used a visual detection system to compare the early stages of the processing of face-related information in young excessive Internet users by analyzing their EEGs. By presenting subjects with images of both faces and objects, the researchers discovered that the brain waves elicited by the viewing of faces were generally larger and peaked sooner than those elicited by the viewing of objects, meaning that the faces had more significance for the viewers than the objects. However, excessive Internet users had a smaller brain-wave response than normal subjects whether they were looking at faces or at chairs, suggesting that for heavy Internet users, faces were perilously close to being of the same physiological importance to them as inanimate objects.

Without the capacity to genuinely communicate with someone through adequate facial recognition cues, it seems almost certain that one will feel less free to express oneself to others in the non-virtual world due to the uncertainty over what the other person is thinking or feeling. Therefore, in the same way that the need to be in agreement with another person is being conditioned into us by social media, the lack of certainty in relating to others created by an unnecessary need to read the faces of other people while one is communicating with them in cyberspace might inevitably cause us to be less free even when we are offline—victims of our own increasing uncertainty in relating to and communicating with others.

Since the time of Jean-Paul Sartre, Albert Camus, and Simone de Beauvoir, when the new philosophy of freedom known as existentialism entered the modern world following the various horrors of fascism that emerged during the mid-twentieth century, the idea of absolute free choice has had a powerful impact on people as they awoke to the idea that one is not necessarily bound by one's own conditioning.

Yet after a brief period of rapid cultural change during the 1950s through the 1970s, when many people embraced that freedom by throwing off many of the social and psychological constraints to which those of previous generations had succumbed, the ever-present need to conform to society's dictates, either directly or indirectly, began to once again rear its ugly head as societies soon made true existential freedom increasingly difficult to achieve by becoming ever more homogenous and the pressure to conform became ever greater.

Now, with the emergence of the Internet and the advent of a digital age that is increasingly swallowing more and more people not only by conditioning the way people think and relate to others by predetermined algorithms inside powerful search engines but also by itself becoming the sort of restrictive barrier that it is becoming increasingly impossible to exist outside of if one wishes to communicate with other people—a type of final stake, it seems, may now be in the process of being driven into the heart of people's capacity to be existentially free.

In Carlos Castaneda's series of books, the Yaqui Indian Don Juan, who had become Castaneda's spiritual adviser in his attempt to become a man of knowledge, referred to the people of the world who condition us with their false views on what is real and what is not as "black magicians." Unfortunately, this may very much be what the Internet and digital age has become for many of us—a black magician of sorts that leads us to believe we are becoming freer to express ourselves, seek knowledge, and communicate more effectively with others when in fact just the opposite may be the case.

Even though everyone is now able to communicate directly and immediately with all sorts of people with whom one couldn't possibly do so as late as thirty years ago, before everyone possessed PCs and smartphones, our communication with others has gotten shallower even as it has expanded and grown wider. That is, in the past, because people by necessity had to communicate with others in person, by phone, or by letter, those communications tended not only to be more personal but also to possess significantly more depth than the present-day communications by email or text messaging, which have become more and more the norm. While the latter are obviously more convenient, at the same time they are shallower forms of communication, meaning ironically a greater loss of personal freedom for all of us simply because the parameters of that communication have shrunk significantly.

As one is forced to communicate by typing words into a digital screen in the form of text messaging or email, where longer versions of these types of communication often begin to appear as strange or overly wordy, or by putting one's thoughts into the recently revised 280 characters on Twitter, the clarity of what one is attempting to communicate to someone else is significantly constricted by the need for brevity.

As a result, within such forms of communication where brevity is at a premium, shortened, edited versions of what one really means to say have rapidly become the accepted norm rather than the exception, with personal freedom of expression being constricted and inhibited, even as we may not realize that this is what is occurring.

Even more dangerously, it is easy to see how our very patterns of thought, the ways in which we conceptualize problems or situations, might tend to become conditioned by this more constricted form of communication with others in the digital world. Over time, we may habitually adopt narrower views of the dynamics of our life, its actual parameters, whether we are doing so on the Internet or in the real world simply because we have become habituated to adopt this more limited apprehension of situations and of other people by the need for abbreviated communication in cyberspace.

In addition, we may even become constrained by the skills of the person with whom we are communicating in the digital world. John Suler, professor of psychology at Rider University, who has written extensively about the behavior of people online, points out in *The Psychology of Cyberspace* that "the quality of the relationship between e-mail correspondents rests on their writing skills." Consequently, if the person with whom one is communicating is doing so ineffectively or inaccurately, people will tend to project their own expectations, anxieties, and fantasies onto the other person. Over time, if someone has enough of these inaccurate encounters in cyberspace to which

Suler is referring, it is easy to see how their own worldview might become increasingly misplaced and narrower.

As with any new technology, particularly one as startling and dramatic as the Internet with all its digital devices, an obvious fascination sets in that only grows as new forms of that technology increasingly appear. And, of course, it is nothing short of fascinating how the Internet has dramatically connected our world in ways we never thought possible, bringing all of us exponentially closer together.

Yet, at the same time, it would seem that so many people are failing to see one basic, potentially dangerous aspect of this new cyber world—namely, that as we are able to use it to connect with our larger world more easily and effectively, we are becoming increasingly constrained within some rather specific boundaries, those which become even harder to apprehend due to the very effects that our digital world is having on our minds, brains, and awareness.

Indeed, it is these very boundaries that can easily become impediments to pursuing the type of larger consciousness that requires, as much as anything, a delicate, creative, subtlety of mind, a number of them having already been addressed in this particular work.

Even though few people may be genuinely concerned with this issue—how the Internet and digital age may be impediments to this search for a larger intelligence that might exist on the other side of our thinking minds—that doesn't mean that the cyber world in which we live isn't necessarily still having its deleterious effects on the possibility of that search. So this is where we will journey next—how to live in and use our cyber world while, at the same time, not allowing it to become a potential psychological barrier to achieving the sort of larger awareness of which we are all capable, even if so few of us actually choose to pursue it.

Chapter Eleven

Consciousness in Cyberspace

How does cyberspace, with all its digital devices, impact the search for an expanded consciousness at a deeply psychological level?

This is certainly not an easy question to answer, and one that this book has attempted to address even as the question itself does not yet fully exist in the modern world. That is, it is now on very few people's radar screens relative to such issues as how the Internet might be affecting people's attention spans as it creates a distracted awareness in them—the effect that the multitasking in which so many people are now engaged might be compromising their capacity to be creative—or how their obsessive use of smartphones might be affecting people's emotive lives.

Of course, all three of these issues ultimately affect how people who wish to do so might pursue some type of enlightened awareness. Yet, so far, the next step toward this issue hasn't yet been taken. Perhaps that's because writers and thinkers like Krishnamurti, Carlos Castaneda, Alan Watts, or Aldous Huxley are not read as much as they used to be some forty or fifty years ago. And so the idea of consciousness expansion may unfortunately have been significantly forgotten as an increasing number of people seem to be concerning themselves largely with political issues or social change.

Yet if the modern world is to ever come to grips with how our new cyber age might be affecting human consciousness, it is going to necessarily need to start focusing directly on this issue, meaning that the emphasis on the inner life that was so much a part of our culture during the middle part of the twentieth century (when young people were so deeply concerned with the writings of authors like Friedrich Nietzsche, Hemann Hesse, or Jack Kerouac) might need to return in full force so that we might all develop a better perspective on how our digital devices might be affecting us at a deeper level.

In other words, change is going to have to come from the top down, so to speak, by people once again making their inner lives more important than their convenient (and often endlessly interesting) use of new technologies— technologies that in the past, although certainly necessary and important, had certain unintended consequences.

For instance, with the invention of the printing press in the fifteenth century, and the exponential increase in the number of books that followed, although masses of people could educate themselves in a manner that couldn't be imagined previously, young people who couldn't read no longer had access to the same information adults did. So then, because information and knowledge was now transmitted primarily through the written word rather than just orally, children could no longer share in adult life to the same degree they did previously.

In response to this situation, the modern school was created so that young people could be more connected to adult society. However, as a result of this separation of childhood and adulthood into increasingly separate psychological categories and worlds, children began to be shut out of the world of work, commerce, and adult life in which they had previously been able to participate. So, as a result, the printing press, as important an invention as it was, served to significantly separate young people from the adult world.

Television also had certain unanticipated, less-than-healthy consequences for everyone. Although, like the Internet, it provided people with information about the world, and significantly increased the possibilities for how they could be entertained, it likewise served to separate people, particularly members of families, from each other. Whereas previously family members or groups of friends might have sat with each other quietly while conversing, read to each other, or ended up doing the family chores together, with the advent of television, although people still sat together in the same room, they were significantly separated simply because they were each exclusively focused on the television screen in front of them, rather than on each other.

Now, in our modern Internet age, a similar dynamic of unanticipated, unintended consequences may likewise be occurring. Even with our capacity to connect with others at lightning speed and our ability to have immediate access to information at a rate that would have been unheard of even thirty or forty years ago, our ability to attend and concentrate, our emotive lives, and our capacity for creative thought might be at the same time negatively affected in ways in which we're not yet fully aware, enamored as we are with how quickly we can retrieve information and knowledge and how much easier it is to connect with others, even those on the other side of the world.

A large part of the problem may simply be that the outer world of utilitarian concerns relative to commerce, education, social and political concerns, or even the arts themselves seems to have become more important than the inner-directed world, with its explorations of consciousness, human psychology, or the hidden dynamics of interpersonal relations.

The Millennial generation appears to be very much concerned with "changing the world," as the saying goes, with many Millennials focusing on politics and social activism, rather than on an understanding that if one attempts to focus exclusively on changing the course of human events—rather than on Alan Watts's *stream of life*, to which one needs to necessarily surrender if one is to uncover any real truths about the nature of oneself or the world—one may end up inherently in conflict with oneself. At the same time, in so doing, one would be led further away from the basic truth that we are all conditioned products of our world.

In education, rather than focusing on the actual life of the child while he or she is being schooled, as many education writers such as George Dennison or A.S. Neill advocated some forty or fifty years ago, schools and educators now tend to focus exclusively on external results of learning such as grades and test scores, without understanding that a results-driven approach to learning inevitably leads to dulled, disembodied experience within the inner lives of young people in their formative years.

Even our arts appear to be succumbing to the outer world of action and human behavior rather than the inner world of consciousness articulated by such writers as Virginia Woolf or Marcel Proust. It was only fifteen years ago that the brilliant movie *The Hours*, which focused on Woolf's inner life relative to the inner lives of two other women living in different time periods, appeared in movie theaters. Yet amid the current glut of female action movies like those that are part of *The Hunger Games* or *Divergent* series, one still waits for another brilliant, inner-directed feminine movie like *The Hours* to once again appear.

Of course, the appearance of the Internet itself has likewise had an enormous effect on this trend away from the inner-directed life toward an outer-directed world that focuses primarily on human behavior and external results simply because communication in cyberspace, no matter how specific and personal it might become, is necessarily a connection that is taking place between people at arm's length from each other, one that doesn't take place in person in the real world of events and interpersonal connections as people relate to each other more and more behind the safe enclave of their plastic screens.

Consequently, because people can somehow remain at arm's length from each other while communicating in cyberspace, the emotive inner life inherent in the realm of interpersonal connection that takes place in the real world may be significantly under assault. And as this continues to increasingly occur, the focus in all different aspects of our world, from commerce to education to the arts, will almost certainly continue to be outer directed and behaviorally oriented, as opposed to inner directed and psychologically oriented.

An inner-directed life is, of course, the one necessary ingredient for pursuing a larger consciousness. Yet, at the same time, that inner-directed life is highly dependent on one's capacity to attend and focus with a certain level of intensity, on being able to react to events in one's life with his or her emotive life completely engaged, on the internal mapping of one's engagements with his or her external environment fully intact so that inner and outer worlds might eventually be experienced as one, and on one's capacity to read or listen to others in conversation at a genuinely deep level of interest.

Unfortunately, as has been articulated in other parts of this work, those very capacities may be in danger of being compromised by people's absorption in the Internet and their addictive use of digital devices in ways that affect at one and the same time their ability to attend, the potential richness of their inner lives, and their capacity for creative thought as their awareness becomes increasingly distracted and their emotive lives grow ever more dulled and disembodied.

Much of this has yet to be scientifically proved in a way that might cause educators, writers, psychologists, lawmakers, or others to take some sort of preventative action. Yet, in terms of the subject of this work, the potential effects of the Internet age and people's use of digital devices on the possibility of achieving a larger, more expansive awareness, it would appear that there are already some rather self-evident truths.

One, of course, is the already well-documented dynamic that people's engagement with the technologies of the cyber world is leaving many with a distracted awareness and a more limited attention span. The Internet's endless supply of relentless, fast-moving information that comes at us daily prevents our minds from focusing as fully or creatively as they otherwise might as information and knowledge passes through our working memories at a speed that often makes it nearly impossible for us to fully grasp that with which we are coming into contact.

In addition, what is most disturbing about this development is how rapidly it can occur in people, and how permanent the changes to their brains can become. In *The Shallows*, Nicholas Carr recounts an experiment conducted by Gary Small, a professor of psychiatry at UCLA in 2008, the first of its kind, which actually showed how quickly people's brains can change in response to Internet use.

Studying the brains of experienced Web surfers and novices as both groups scanned Google, the scans revealed that the Internet-savvy subjects used a specific network in the left front part of their brain while the brains of the Internet-naïve subjects showed minimal, if any, activity in this same area. Yet six days later, after the researchers had the Internet-naïve group spend just an hour a day online, they found that the same neural circuitry found to exist in the brains of the experienced Web surfers was now showing up in the brains of the previously inexperienced Internet users. In other words, just an hour a day for six days was all it took to begin rewiring their brains in a manner similar to how the brains of those who had been regular Internet users had already been rewired.

In addition, when the researchers studied the difference in brain activity between those who read webpages and those who read books, they found that those who surfed the Web exhibited a very different pattern of brain activity than when they read a book. Book readers had significant activity in regions of the brain associated with language, memory, and visual processing, but they didn't display activity in the brain's prefrontal regions associated with decision making and problem solving, while Web users displayed activity across all regions of the brain while they scanned and searched webpages.

Although one may look at this measurement of brain activity as being a positive for extensive Internet users, it in fact may not be. What it demonstrates is that as Web users can so easily become physiologically habituated to making choices about where they will navigate next while they are online, that same constant decision-making process may be exactly what prevents them from sinking into an article or other piece of text while they are online, as they would if they were simply reading a book, magazine, or newspaper.

If it's true, as it increasingly appears to be, that our brains are actually being rewired to become more effective at how we use the Internet, even as they become less able to focus attentively on our thoughts or the details of our world, or to sink into a piece of writing or an extended conversation, then that is something that is almost certainly going to prove to be more than a little deleterious for the arduous task of examining our thinking minds in search of a limitless reality that may lie beyond them.

In addition, the deleterious effects that our cyber age might be having upon people's emotive lives is something that needs to be considered just as carefully as the effects of people's use of their digital devices on their cognitive lives.

As has been alluded to throughout this work, the inorganic images that people are apprehending daily on their plastic screens, in lieu of a fuller participation in the details of the real world, are going to leave a certain amount of dulled, disembodied experience within them simply because those virtual images don't allow for the same level of impressionistic depth that real-world events and interactions with others do. As a result of this inorganic interaction, the sort of emotive intelligence necessary to probing the inner world in search of something larger may become less available.

Unfortunately, relative to this flattening of experience in the cyber world are the compulsive loops of digital addiction in which people who go online or use their phones consistently can easily find themselves as they potentially flood their brains with powerful neurotransmitters like dopamine while habitually posting on social media, sending text messages, or compulsively checking their email for new messages, or Facebook and Twitter for new likes.

As the intense stimulation of images moving across one's computer screen or phone produces a habitual, addictive excitement, the person addicted to digital technology and the Internet seeks to reward himself further by posting, tweeting, texting, emailing, or merely surfing the Web. Then, as they become ever more willing victims of this addictive cycle, the sterile images on their plastic screen captivate them all the more, thus flattening their inner lives even further.

Regardless of what one may think about the entrance of the Internet into all our lives, this addiction to inorganic images and flattened, sterile experience is very real indeed. It accounts for the results of the experiment alluded to above, in which those who suffered from Internet addiction demonstrated the same brain waves in response to looking at either a chair or a human face. Very likely, the positive sensations they experienced as a result of their digital compulsion had become just as important to them as the feelings that may have been engendered in them by looking at the face.

The point is that people's emotive inner lives are almost certainly being flattened by living in a virtual world in which they increasingly live, and unless something appears to counteract that trend, their sensorial apprehensions of the world will move increasingly further from being able to experience the miraculous, intimate details of it with the same depth that those such as Henry David Thoreau or Walt Whitman were able to achieve.

And as their sensorial lives grow increasingly deadened, they will likewise move further away from the possibility of being able to use their visual sense to experience the infinite in a vase of flowers, as Aldous Huxley was able to do during his experience with mescaline (only doing so without needing to use some drug to stimulate their visual sense).

There is also the extremely troubling possibility that the natural flow of our thoughts is being increasingly directed and impeded by the virtual networks inside our computers or phones, not to mention, as was discussed earlier, how people are outsourcing their working memories, those which engender logic and creative thinking, to powerful search engines like Google or powerful virtual devices like the memory facilitator Echo. As a result, our minds are becoming more conditioned than they have ever been simply because the conditioning, rather than existing in the dynamics and forces of one's exterior world, is now largely interior.

Once our thinking mind comes under the control of the algorithms that are part of powerful search engines or websites, we increasingly lose the ability to stand back and apprehend how the natural flow of our thoughts might be synonymous with the passage of time simply because that flow is now something that is being directed from outside us. That is, because we are no longer in control of its direction, we lose the capacity to perceive its essential nature.

Understanding how the passage of time and the flow of thought is one and the same process is the first step toward asking whether there is in fact a timeless psychological state with which one might be able to come into contact. And by asking whether there is in fact such a perception that is not part of time and thought—a perception that is entirely outside the patterns that our brains habitually pursue—in that moment one begins to explore the possibility of a limitless consciousness that is not bound by our thinking minds.

Yet if we have begun giving up control of the networks of our thinking minds by outsourcing them to the algorithms that are part of powerful search engines inside our phones and computers as our digital addictions grow, it seems entirely possible that we might never be able to come to such a basic realization about the nature of our thoughts in relation to the passage of time simply because we've lost any genuine capacity for the sort of reflective awareness that can only come about when one is able to step outside the flow of one's own thoughts exactly because one is still in control of them.

There is also the essential indirect subtlety of mind necessary for making such a realization concerning thought and time, and how the extreme rigidity inherent in the cyber world may be likewise affecting that. Yes, computers can access information and knowledge probably faster than we humans ever will, and they are probably even better at solving complex, difficult problems, even ones that necessitate highly creative solutions. Yet they will never possess the ability to be truly reflective and self-conscious, and that is their one extreme limitation relative to putting ourselves in touch with a larger intelligence.

Of course, unlike us humans, these are inorganic beings, which means that they possess no emotive, impressionistic life whatsoever even if we continually feed them our own emotive lives on social media or the websites we create. And intelligence, in its purest form, is much more a matter of integrating our emotive, impressionistic lives with our thoughts than it is a matter of solving technical problems or retrieving information and knowledge more quickly than it has previously been retrieved.

The most profound danger that the Internet and all our digital devices represent isn't even the distracted awareness that is being engendered in so many of us, or the flattening of our emotive experience and inner lives. It's the potential deleterious effects that the cyber world may be having on our minds and brains relative to seeking an expansive consciousness that lies beyond the boundaries of the self, even though it's probably only a tiny number of people in the world who will ever end up pursuing such a thing.

Yet for enough people to come to that realization so that things might begin to possibly change means that political and social causes, the pursuit of money, celebrity, or socially sanctioned success must begin to assume their proper place relative to the actual reason why we inhabit planet earth for such a brief period of time—namely, to pursue the truth of our existence by attempting to put ourselves in touch with an infinity from which our life energy originates.

Not only does the Web, with all its accompanying technologies, make such a pursuit more difficult by its effects on our cognitive and emotive processes, but it also makes it more difficult exactly because such a larger consciousness is veritably impossible to achieve in cyberspace when the extreme subtlety of mind necessary for doing so begins to disappear. Consequently, in our digitally consumed world, the search for a more integrated intelligence begins to literally vanish from view as we continue to surrender to the rigid nature of algorithms and coding.

Of course, the digital world has its place in giving us the amazing technologies that allow us to connect with each other and retrieve information and knowledge at a speed that would have been unimaginable only a few decades ago. Yet, unfortunately, our cyber world might easily become more and more a reality in which we ourselves come to resemble the two passengers on the spaceship inside Stanley Kubrick's brilliant movie *2001: A Space Odyssey* as they surrendered themselves to the will of Hal, the futuristic computer under whose control they increasingly found themselves.

In addition, what is truly frightening about this development is the way that the cyber world has crept into all our lives without us even being aware of how it has done so as we become increasingly fascinated by the power of the Web, the magic of smartphones and iPods, or simply the incredible interconnectedness that Facebook or other social media sites provide without stopping to ask the provocative questions of what effects these things might be having on our networks of thought, our inner lives, the nature of interpersonal relationships, our physiological brains, or even our personal freedom.

When Nicholas Carr wrote *The Shallows*, he was referring to the shallow world we enter as we go online and find ourselves skipping through websites, skimming articles, habitually posting on social media in a manner often devoid of depth of thought or nuance, or continually interrupting our attention spans to check our text messages and emails. Yet, in a sense, he might have unknowingly likewise been referring to the shallowness of so many people in our world who have become so fascinated and enticed by the Web and the digital devices necessary for navigating cyberspace that they don't stop to really consider what deleterious effects this radical new digital world with its almost magical technologies might be having on them.

Once again, Neil Postman said it: What problems does any new technology solve, and what new problems does it create? These are without a doubt two questions worth asking in this new fascinating, dangerous cyber world that we have all now come to inhabit or, for those of a younger generation, were born into without much knowledge of the possibilities that might exist beyond it.

Appendix

QUALITIES OF INTELLIGENCE POTENTIALLY
COMPROMISED BY THE DIGITAL AGE

1. Fully focused attention
2. Full access to one's working memories (both short and long term)
3. Capacity for direct insight into situations and people
4. Ability to think creatively
5. A vibrant emotive life
6. Capacity for developing a clear internal picture of one's world
7. Capacity for deep thought and reading
8. Ability to explore the boundaries of thought and memory
9. Capacity for achieving a mental "flow" state that is creative
10. Access to truths that great art and literature represent
11. A capacity to examine one's conditioning through self-reflection

Bibliography

Alban, Deane. "Serotonin Deficiency: Signs, Symptoms, Solutions." https://bebrainfit.com/serotonin-deficiency/.

Addiction.com. "Technology Addiction." https://www.addiction.com/addiction-a-to-z/technology-addiction/.

Allen, Summer. "The Multitasking Mind." October 9, 2013. https://www.brainfacts.org/thinking-sensing-and-behaving/thinking-and-awareness/2013/the-multitasking-mind.

Anderson, Pauline. "Brain Abnormalities Linked to Internet Addiction." *Medscape*, May 5, 2014.

Aubri, John. "OCD & Dopamine." https://www.livestrong.com/article/307232-ocd-dopamine/.

Bakewell, Sarah. *At the Existentialist Café*. New York: Other Press, 2016.

Bauerlein, Mark. *The Dumbest Generation: How the Digital Age Stupefies Young Americans and Jeopardizes Our Future (Or Don't Trust Anyone under 30)*. New York: Penguin Group, 2008.

Baym, Nancy K. *Personal Connections in the Digital Age*. Cambridge: Polity Press, 2015.

Bipeta, Raishekhar, Srinivasa Yerramilli, Ashok Reddy Karredla, and Srinath Gopinath. "Diagnostic Stability of Internet Addiction in Obsessive-Compulsive Disorder: Data from a Naturalistic One-Year Treatment Study." *Innovations in Clinical Neuroscience* 12, nos. 3–4 (March–April 2015): 14–23.

Blau, Evelyne. *Krishnamurti: 100 Years*. New York: A Joost Elffers Book, 1995.

Bohm, David. *Wholeness and the Implicate Order*. London: Routledge, 1980.

Bouchez, Colette. "Serotonin: 9 Questions and Answers." https://www.webmd.com/depression/features/serotonin#1.

Bradberry, Travis, and Jean Greaves. *Emotional Intelligence 2.0*. San Diego: Talent Smart, 2009.

Capra, Fritjof. *The Tao of Physics*. Boston: Shambala, 1975.

Carr, Nicholas. "Is Google Making Us Stupid?" *The Atlantic* (July/August 2008).

———. *The Shallows: What the Internet Is Doing to Our Brains*. New York: W.W. Norton, 2011, 2010.

Castenada, Carlos. *Tales of Power*. New York: Simon & Schuster, 1974.

Castro, Joseph. "Sea Slug Offers Clues to Improving Long-Term Memory." *Live Science*, December 30, 2011.

Chandler, Paul, and John Sweller. "Cognitive Load Theory and the Format of Instruction." *Cognition and Instruction* 8, no. 4 (1991): 293–332.

Cowan, Nelson. *Attention and Memory: An Integrated Framework.* New York: Oxford University Press, 1998.

Csikszentmihalyi, Mihaly. *Creativity: Flow and the Psychology of Discovery and Invention.* New York: HarperCollins, 1996.

Davidow, Bill. "Exploring the Neuroscience of Internet Addiction." *The Atlantic* (July 2012).

Davidson, Cathy. *Now You See It: How the Brain Science of Attention Will Transform the Way We Live, Work and Learn.* New York: Viking Press, 2011.

Eichenbaum, H. "Time Cells in the Hippocampus: A New Dimension for Mapping Memories." *Nature Reviews Neuroscience* 15, no. 11 (2014): 732–44.

Frankl, Victor E. *Man's Search for Meaning.* Boston: Beacon Press, 1959.

Gazzaley, Adam, and Larry D. Rosen.*The Distracted Mind: Ancient Brains in a High-Tech World.* Cambridge, MA: MIT Press, 2016.

Gekoski, Rick. "What's the Definition of a Great Book?" *The Guardian*, December 23, 2011.

Goleman, Daniel. *Emotional Intelligence*. New York: Bantam Books, 1995.

Greenfield, Susan. *Mind Change: How Digital Technologies Are Leaving Their Marks on Our Brain.* New York: Random House, 2015.

Gregoire, Carolyn. "How Technology Is Warping Your Memory." *Huffington Post.* Updated January 25, 2014.

Grugier, Maxence. "The Digital Age of Data Art." May 8, 2016. https://techcrunch.com/2016/05/08/the-digital-age-of-data-art/.

Harris, B. "A Letter to Someone with Obsessive Compulsive Disorder." December 10, 2010.

Harrison, Robert Pogue. "The True American." *New York Review of Books*, August 17, 2017.

Hesse, Hermann. *Siddartha.* New York: New Directions, 1951.

Holroyd, Stuart. *Krishnamurti: The Man, the Mystery, and the Message.* Delhi, India: New Age Books, 1991.

Huth, John. "Losing Our Way in the World." *New York Times*, July 20, 2013.

Huxley, Aldous. *The Doors of Perception.* New York: HarperCollins, 1954.

Insel, Thomas R. "Serotonin in Obsessive Compulsive Order." *Psychiatric Annals* 20 (October 1990).

Isaacson, Andy. "Learning to Let Go: First Turn Off the Phone." *New York Times*, December 14, 2012.

Jaynes, Julian. *The Origin of Consciousness in the Breakdown of the Bicameral Mind.* New York: Houghton Mifflin Harcourt, 1976, 1990.

Kandel, Eric R. *In Search of Memory.* New York: W.W. Norton, 2006.

———. *The Age of Insight: The Quest to Understand the Unconscious in Art, Mind, and Brain.* New York: Random House, 2012.

Karderas, Nicholas. "It's Digital Heroin: How Screens Turn Kids into Psychotic Junkies." *New York Post*, August 27, 2016.

Kim, C. H., M. S. Koo, K. A. Cheon, Y. H. Ryu, J. D. Lee, and H. S. Lee. "Dopamine Transporter Density of Basal Ganglia." *European Journal of Nuclear Medicine and Molecular Imaging*, December 10, 2010.

Kounios, John, and Mark Jung-Beeman. "The Aha! Moment: The Cognitive Neuroscience of Insight." *APS: A Journal of the Association for Psychological Science* (2009).

Krishnamurti, J. *The Awakening of Intelligence.* New York: HarperCollins, 1973.

———. *The Wholeness of Life.* New York: Harper & Row, 1979.

Laing, Olivia. "The Future of Loneliness." *The Guardian*, April 1, 2015.

Laing, R. D. *The Divided Self.* New York: Penguin, 1969.

Lehrer, Jonah. *Proust Was a Neuroscientist.* Boston/New York: Houghton-Mifflin, 2007.

Levitin, Daniel J. *The Organized Mind.* New York: Plume, 2014.

Lewin, Tamar. "As Interest Fades in the Humanities, Colleges Worry." *New York Times*, October 30, 2013.

Marquize, Kelly. "Dopamine and OCD: The Role that Dopamine Plays in OCD." December 13, 2010. https://www.healthguideinfo.com/types-of-ocd/p99037/.

McLuhan, Marshall. *Understanding Media: The Extension of Man.* Critical edition edited by W. Terrence Gordon. Corte Madera, CA: Gingko Press, 2003.

Metivier, Anthony. "Serotonin: The Truth You Need for Memory Improvement" (podcast). September 7, 2016.

Metz, Cade. "AI Is Transforming Google Search. The Rest of the Web Is Next." February 4, 2016. https://www.wired.com/2016/02/ai-is-changing-the-technology-behind-google-searches/.

Meyer, David, and D. E. Kieras. "A Computational Theory of Executive Cognitive Processes and Multiple-Task Performance: Parts 1 and 2." *Psychological Review* 104, no. 1 (1997): 3–65.

Mills, Kathryn L. "Possible Effects of Internet Use on Cognitive Development in Adolescence." *Media and Communication* 4, issue 3 (2016): 4–12.

Moody, David Edmund. *An Uncommon Collaboration: David Bohm and J. Krishnamurti.* Ojai, CA: Alpha Centauri Press, 2016.

Nass, Clifford. *Proceeding of the National Academy of Sciences.* 2009 study.

"The Negative Impacts of Social Media on Face-to-Face Interactions." *Final Inquiry Project*, December 1, 2015. https://rampages.us/peasedn200/2015/12/01/final-inquiry-project/.

Olvera-Cortes, M. E., P. Anguiano-Rodriguez, M. A. Lopez-Vazquez, and J. M. Alfar. "Serotonin/Dopamine Interaction in Learning." *Progress in Brain Research* 172 (2008): 567–602.

Palladino, Lucy Jo. *Find Your Focus Zone: An Effective New Plan to Defeat Distraction and Overload.* New York: Free Press, 2007.

Paul, Annie Murphy. "The New Marshmallow Test: Resisting the Temptations of the Web." May 3, 2013. https://hechingerreport.org/the-new-marshmallow-test-resisting-the-temptations-of-the-web/.

———. "Who's Afraid of Digital Natives?" Slate.com, August 2011.

Piaget, Jean, and Barbel Inhelder. *The Psychology of the Child.* Translated by Helen Weaver. New York: Basic Books, 1969.

Poldrack, Russell. Proceedings of the National Academy of Sciences. 2006 study.

Postman, Neil. *The Disappearance of Childhood.* New York: Vintage Books, 1982.

Preston, Alison. "How Does Short-Term Memory Work in Relation to Long-Term Memory? Are Short-Term Daily Memories Somehow Transferred to Long-Term Storage while We Sleep?" *Scientific American*, March 9, 2017.

Proust, Marcel. *In Search of Lost Time (Remembrance of Things Past).* France: Grasset and Gallimard, 1913–1927.

Ramasubbu, Suren. "Does Technology Impact a Child's Emotional Intelligence?" *Huffington Post*, April 20, 2015.

Randolph, Elizabeth. "Distracted Reading in the Digital Age." *Vassar: The Almanae/i Quarterly* 111, issue 1 (Winter 2015).

Robbins, Martin. "Mind Change: Susan Greenfield Has a Big Idea, but What Is It?" *The Guardian*, October 3, 2014.

Sartre, Jean-Paul. *Nausea.* New York: New Directions, 1964.

Schiller, Daniela, et al. "Memory and Space: Toward an Understanding of the Cognitive Map." *Journal of Neuroscience* 35, no. 41 (October 14, 2015): 13904–11.

Schwartz, Tony. *The Way We're Working Isn't Working.* New York: Free Press, 2010.

"Serotonin and Dopamine." December 15, 2016. https://www.newhealthadvisor.org/Serotonin-and-Dopamine.html.

Sheremata, Summer L., and Michael A. Silver. "Hemisphere-Dependent Attentional Modulation of Human Parietal Visual Field Representations." *Journal of Neuroscience* 35, no. 2 (January 14, 2015): 508–17.

Sherff, Carolyn, and Thomas Carew. "A Role for Serotonin in Long-Term Memory." *Yale Medicine* 34, no. 2 (Spring 2000).

Shirahata, Takaai, Makoto Tsunoda, Tomofum Santa, Yutaka Kirino, and Satoshi Watanabe. "Depletion of Serotonin Selectively Impairs Short-Term Memory without Affecting Long-Term Memory in Odor Learning in the Terrestrial Slug 'Limax Valentianus.'" *Learning and Memory* 13, no. 3 (May–June 2006): 267–70.

Sparrow, Betsy, Jenny Liu, and Daniel M. Wegner. "Google Effects on Memory: Cognitive Consequences of Having Information at Our Fingertips." *Science* 333, issue 6043 (August 5, 2011): 776–78.

Stibel, Jeff. "Why the Internet Is So Distracting (And What You Can Do about It)." *Harvard Business Review*, October 20, 2009.

Stoll, Clifford. *Silicon Snake Oil: Second Thoughts on the Information Highway.* New York: Anchor Books, 1995.

Suler, John. "E-Mail Communication and Relationships." *The Psychology of Cyberspace.* 1996. http://truecenterpublishing.com/psycyber/emailrel.html.

Swanson, Jeanene. "The Neurological Basis for Digital Addiction." October 6, 2014. https://www.thefix.com/content/digital-addictions-are-real-addictions.

Thoreau, Henry David. *Walden; Or Life in the Woods.* Boston: Ticknor and Fields, 1854.

Thurlow, Crispin, Laura Lengel, and Alice Tomic. *Computer Mediated Communication.* London: Sage, 2004.

Turkle, Sherry. *Alone Together: Why We Expect More from Technology and Less from Each Other.* New York: Basic Books, 2012.

Twenge, Jean M. "Has the Smartphone Destroyed a Generation?" *The Atlantic* (September 2017).

Watts, Alan W. *The Wisdom of Insecurity.* New York: Pantheon Books, 1951.

Wegner, Daniel M., and Adrian F. Ward. "The Internet Has Become the External Hard Drive for Our Memories." *Scientific American*, December 1, 2013.

White, Michael, and John Gribbin. *Stephen Hawking: A Life in Science.* Washington, DC: Joseph Henry Press, 1992.

Whitman, Walt. *Leaves of Grass.* Brooklyn: James and Andrew Rome, 1855.

Williams, Simon J. "Emotions, Cyberspace and the 'Virtual' Body: A Critical Appraisal." In *Emotions in Social Life: Critical Themes and Contemporary Issues*, edited by Gillian Bendelow and Simon J. Williams. London: Routledge, 1998.

Wolf, Fred Alan. *Taking the Quantum Leap: The New Physics for Non-Scientists.* New York: HarperCollins, 1981.

Wolf, Maryanne. *Proust and the Squid: The Story and Science of the Reading Brain.* New York: HarperCollins, 2007.

Wolpert, Stuart. "Is Technology Producing a Decline in Critical Thinking and Analysis?" January 27, 2009. http://newsroom.ucla.edu/releases/is-technology-producing-a-decline-79127.

Index

Gekoski, Rick, 57
Goleman, Daniel, 69
Google, 92–93, 103. *See also* algorithms
Greaves, Jean, 68–69
Greenfield, David, 14
Greenfield, Patricia, 46–47
Greenfield, Susan, 11, 15, 41, 95

Harris, Bill, 18
Harrison, Robert Pogue, 66
Hawking, Stephen, 76
Hebb, Donald O., 63
Heidegger, Martin, 29
Heisenberg, Werner, 26, 51
Hesse, Hermann, 84
hippocampus, 21, 23, 81
humanities studies, 53–54
Husserl, Edmund, 29
Huth, John, 10
Huxley, Aldous, 22, 30, 82

identity, Internet addiction and, 15
imagination, Internet/digital age and, 59
implicit memories, 21, 91
impressionistic depth. *See* emotive lives
information retrieval, Internet/digital age
    and, 2, 8. *See also* outsourcing of
    memory
inner life: and art appreciation, 69; and
    consciousness expansion, 81;
    importance of, 100; Internet/digital age
    and, 101–102
insight, 63–73; Internet/digital age and, 65,
    67–68, 69, 109; literature and, 70;
    physiological basis of, 63; and sense of
    space, 83
intelligence, 106; and insight, 64; qualities
    of, Internet/digital age and, 109;
    working memory and, 38
Internet addiction, 13–23; and anxiety,
    78–79; and confirmation bias, 15,
    16–17; and dopamine, 13–14; and
    emotive lives, 104–105
Internet/digital age, 1–4; and art and
    culture, 53–61; and attention, 43–52;
    benefits of, 2–3; and cognitive issues,
    5–11; and consciousness expansion,
    99–107; and creativity, 43–52;
    disadvantages of, 3, 23, 31, 33–34; and

freedom, 87–98; as insidious, 107; and
    insight, 65, 67–68, 69, 109; and sense
    of space and time, 75–85; unintended
    consequences of, 100–101
Internet Use Disorder (IUD), 18. *See also*
    Internet addiction
interneurons, 40
intuition, Internet/digital age and, 4
iPhone, 1, 2. *See also* cell phones; Internet/
    digital age
irrelevant information, and cognitive load,
    20, 37
isolation: Internet/digital age and, 18–19;
    sense of space and, 79–80; television
    and, 100

James, William, 59–60
Jaynes, Julian, 75
Jobs, Steve, 2
Jung-Beeman, Mark, 46, 63, 64

Kafka, Franz, 29
Kandel, Eric, 40, 63
Kerouac, Jack, 69, 70, 71
knowledge: and creativity, 44;
    fragmentation of, 10, 45, 69–70; versus
    intelligence, 64; nature of, 25, 26
Konrath, Sara H., 68
Kounios, John, 46, 63
Krishnamurti, Jiddu, 3, 27, 28, 32, 51, 90;
    and Bohm, 26; on insight, 64; on
    knowledge, 25–26; on thought, 33, 48;
    on space, 82
Kubrick, Stanley, 107

Laing, Olivia, 80
Laing, R. D., 16, 76, 77
Lao Tzu, 26, 27, 30, 82
learning: Internet/digital age and, 46–47,
    91–93; memory and, 91; styles of, 49;
    trends in, 101
Lehrer, Jonah, 28
Levitin, Daniel J., 14
libraries, Internet/digital age and, 2
literature, 53; appreciation of, Internet/
    digital age and, 54, 55–58, 69–71, 109;
    characteristics of greatness in, 57
Liu, Jenny, 89
Lockard, Joe, 79

About the Author

For twelve years, **Lyn Lesch** was founder and director of the Children's School in Evanston, Illinois, a private, progressive, democratically run school for children six to fourteen years of age. During its existence, the school received widespread attention in both electronic and print media in Chicago as a unique, innovative approach to education.

He is also the author of four books on education reform, all stressing the importance of what occurs inside a child *while* they learn, as opposed to a results-driven approach.

In addition, Lyn has a lifelong interest in the subject of a larger consciousness. He can be found at his author website, http://lynlesch.com, writing and blogging about this area of concern, particularly in terms of the effects that modern technology in the current Internet age is having upon it.